TABLE OF CONTENTS

SECRET KEY #1 - TIME IS YOUR GREATEST ENEMY 6
Pace Yourself 6
SECRET KEY #2 - GUESSING IS NOT GUESSWORK...6
Monkeys Take the Test...6
$5 Challenge 7
SECRET KEY #3 - PRACTICE SMARTER, NOT HARDER 8
Success Strategy...8
SECRET KEY #4 - PREPARE, DON'T PROCRASTINATE..8
SECRET KEY #5 - TEST YOURSELF 8
TOP 20 TEST TAKING TIPS 10
GENERAL STRATEGIES 11
Registering for the NSCA-CPT Licensure Test 15
NSCA-CPT CONTENT...16
NSCA-CPT TESTING COST..16
VOCABULARY: EXERCISE TERMINOLOGY 17
BODY COMPOSITION..22
English Formula..23
Metric Formula 24
MALES VS. FEMALES 24
RESPIRATORY REVIEW..25
ENERGY PRODUCTION 26
ATP—ITS ROLE IN THE BODY; METABOLIC PATHWAYS...26
DETERMINING EXERCISE INTENSITY 27
CIRCULATORY SYSTEM 28
COURSE OF CIRCULATION 29
The Heart 30
Cardiovascular Conditions 31
NUTRITION 32
Nutrients Key Points 37
I. Six Key Nutrients 37
II. Water Key Points 37
III. Protein Key Points ....
IV. Mineral Key Points ....
V. Major Minerals ....
VI. Vitamin Key Points ....
VII. Carbohydrates Key Points..
VIII. Fat Key Points 41
EATING DISORDERS 42
WELLNESS 44
PERFORMANCE 46
ERGOGENIC AIDS 48
AXIAL SKELETON...50
APPENDICULAR SKELETON...51
CHARACTERISTICS OF BONE..52
MAJOR TYPES OF HUMAN BONES...53
JOINTS 53
BONES/JOINTS AND MUSCLES—DESCRIPTIONS; JOINT ACTION; MAJOR MUSCLES;
MOVEMENTS PERFORMED 54
MUSCULAR SYSTEM – KEY POINTS..59
Contraction 60
Types of Muscle Fibers 61
MUSCLES—TYPES; PLANES OF MOVEMENT; ACTION...61
GENERAL PRINCIPLES; DEFINITIONS; ELEMENTS OF TRAINING 62
CIRCUIT TRAINING...67

DETRAINING 68
BREATHING EXERCISES...69
    Diaphragmatic Breathing...69
    Purse Lip Beathing 69
    Natural Breathing..70
STRETCHING EXERCISES 70
EXERCISE TECHNIQUE...**75**
LEVER REVIEW **92**
    KEY MOVEMENT TERMS 97
GAIT CYCLE **98**
FLUID INTAKE RECOMMENDATIONS **100**
THE BASICS – SUMMARY **101**
    ENDURANCE 105
        Moderate Activities..105
        Vigorous Activities 105
    BICYCLING 106
        Cycling Tips...106
KEY FORMULAS...**106**
HEART RATE **106**
FITNESS TIPS **107**
    FITNESS MISCONCEPTIONS..107
    EXERCISE IN THE USA 108
    CLIENT CONSULTATION— 109
    ASSESSMENT; EVALUATION TESTS; FORMS 109
    CLIENT'S HISTORY 110
TESTING FLEXIBILITY...**113**
    PROGRAM PLANNING 114
    ORDER OF EXERCISES 114
    AGE CONSIDERATIONS—GUIDELINES FOR PLANNING ACTIVITIES 114
    HEALTH CONSIDERATIONS—GUIDELINES FOR PLANNING ACTIVITIES; HIGH-RISK CLIENTS
   115
    PREGNANCY CONSIDERATIONS 120
    INJURIES; RISKS; GUIDELINES FOR REDUCING INJURY 121
    STRENGTH AND SAFETY GUIDELINES 128
    SETTING UP A PERSONAL TRAINING BUSINESS...128
TRAINER-CLIENT INTERACTION **130**
WEB LINKS INFO – SPECIFIC EXERCISE REVIEW **130**
ONE REP MAX (1RM) **131**
PRACTICE TEST **133**
    PRACTICE QUESTIONS 133
    ANSWER KEY AND EXPLANATIONS 140
SPECIAL REPORT: WHICH STUDY GUIDES AND PRACTICE TESTS ARE WORTH YOUR TIME?
...147
    PRACTICE TESTS 147
    STUDY GUIDES 147
MUSCULATURE/INNERVATION REVIEW – ARM AND BACK **148**
MUSCULATURE/INNERVATION REVIEW – THE FOREARM **149**
MUSCULATURE/INNERVATION REVIEW – THE HAND.......................................**150**
MUSCULATURE/INNERVATION REVIEW – THE THIGH **151**
MUSCULATURE/INNERVATION REVIEW – THE CALF AND FOOT **152**
CPR REVIEW / CHEAT SHEET **153**
    CONSCIOUS CHOKING 153
    UNCONSCIOUS CHOKING 153
    RESCUE BREATHS 153
AED **154**
SPECIAL REPORT: RECOMMENDED DAILY ALLOWANCES **155**

SPECIAL REPORT: ADDITIONAL BONUS MATERIAL **156**

Secret Key #1 - Time is Your Greatest Enemy

Pace Yourself

Wear a watch. At the beginning of the test, check the time (or start a chronometer on your watch to count the minutes), and check the time after every few questions to make sure you are "on schedule."

If you are forced to speed up, do it efficiently. Usually one or more answer choices can be eliminated without too much difficulty. Above all, don't panic. Don't speed up and just begin guessing at random choices. By pacing yourself, and continually monitoring your progress against your watch, you will always know exactly how far ahead or behind you are with your available time. If you find that you are one minute behind on the test, don't skip one question without spending any time on it, just to catch back up. Take 15 fewer seconds on the next four questions, and after four questions you'll have caught back up. Once you catch back up, you can continue working each problem at your normal pace.

Furthermore, don't dwell on the problems that you were rushed on. If a problem was taking up too much time and you made a hurried guess, it must be difficult. The difficult questions are the ones you are most likely to miss anyway, so it isn't a big loss. It is better to end with more time than you need than to run out of time.
Lastly, sometimes it is beneficial to slow down if you are constantly getting ahead of time. You are always more likely to catch a careless mistake by working more slowly than quickly, and among very high-scoring test takers (those who are likely to have lots of time left over), careless errors affect the score more than mastery of material.

Secret Key #2 - Guessing is not Guesswork

You probably know that guessing is a good idea - unlike other standardized tests, there is no penalty for getting a wrong answer. Even if you have no idea about a question, you still have a 20-25% chance of getting it right.

Most test takers do not understand the impact that proper guessing can have on their score. Unless you score extremely high, guessing will significantly contribute to your final score.

Monkeys Take the Test

What most test takers don't realize is that to insure that 20-25% chance, you have to guess randomly. If you put 20 monkeys in a room to take this test, assuming they answered once per question and behaved themselves, on average they would get 20-25% of the questions correct. Put 20 test takers in the room, and the average will be much lower among guessed questions. Why?

1. The test writers intentionally writes deceptive answer choices that "look" right. A test taker has no idea about a question, so picks the "best looking" answer, which is often wrong. The monkey has no idea what looks good and what doesn't, so will consistently be lucky about 20-25% of the time.
2. Test takers will eliminate answer choices from the guessing pool based on a hunch or intuition. Simple but correct answers often get excluded, leaving a 0% chance of being correct. The monkey has no clue, and often gets lucky with the best choice.

This is why the process of elimination endorsed by most test courses is flawed and detrimental to your performance- test takers don't guess, they make an ignorant stab in the dark that is usually worse than random.

$5 Challenge

Let me introduce one of the most valuable ideas of this course- the $5 challenge:

You only mark your "best guess" if you are willing to bet $5 on it.
You only eliminate choices from guessing if you are willing to bet $5 on it.

Why $5? Five dollars is an amount of money that is small yet not insignificant, and can really add up fast (20 questions could cost you $100). Likewise, each answer choice on one question of the test will have a small impact on your overall score, but it can really add up to a lot of points in the end.

The process of elimination IS valuable. The following shows your chance of guessing it right:

If you eliminate wrong answer choices until only this many answer choices remain:	Chance of getting it correct:
1	100%
2	50%
3	33%

However, if you accidentally eliminate the right answer or go on a hunch for an incorrect answer, your chances drop dramatically: to 0%. By guessing among all the answer choices, you are GUARANTEED to have a shot at the right answer.

That's why the $5 test is so valuable- if you give up the advantage and safety of a pure guess, it had better be worth the risk.

What we still haven't covered is how to be sure that whatever guess you make is truly random. Here's the easiest way:

Always pick the first answer choice among those remaining.

Such a technique means that you have decided, **before you see a single test question**, exactly how you are going to guess- and since the order of choices tells you nothing about which one is correct, this guessing technique is perfectly random.

This section is not meant to scare you away from making educated guesses or eliminating choices- you just need to define when a choice is worth eliminating. The $5 test, along with a pre-defined random guessing strategy, is the best way to make sure you reap all of the benefits of guessing.

Secret Key #3 - Practice Smarter, Not Harder

Many test takers delay the test preparation process because they dread the awful amounts of practice time they think necessary to succeed on the test. We have refined an effective method that will take you only a fraction of the time.

There are a number of "obstacles" in your way to succeed. Among these are answering questions, finishing in time, and mastering test-taking strategies. All must be executed on the day of the test at peak performance, or your score will suffer. The test is a mental marathon that has a large impact on your future.

Just like a marathon runner, it is important to work your way up to the full challenge. So first you just worry about questions, and then time, and finally strategy:

Success Strategy

1. Find a good source for practice tests.
2. If you are willing to make a larger time investment, consider using more than one study guide- often the different approaches of multiple authors will help you "get" difficult concepts.
3. Take a practice test with no time constraints, with all study helps "open book." Take your time with questions and focus on applying strategies.
4. Take a practice test with time constraints, with all guides "open book."
5. Take a final practice test with no open material and time limits

If you have time to take more practice tests, just repeat step 5. By gradually exposing yourself to the full rigors of the test environment, you will condition your mind to the stress of test day and maximize your success.

Secret Key #4 - Prepare, Don't Procrastinate

Let me state an obvious fact: if you take the test three times, you will get three different scores. This is due to the way you feel on test day, the level of preparedness you have, and, despite the test writers' claims to the contrary, some tests WILL be easier for you than others.

Since your future depends so much on your score, you should maximize your chances of success. In order to maximize the likelihood of success, you've got to prepare in advance. This means taking practice tests and spending time learning the information and test taking strategies you will need to succeed.

Never take the test as a "practice" test, expecting that you can just take it again if you need to. Feel free to take sample tests on your own, but when you go to take the official test, be prepared, be focused, and do your best the first time!

Secret Key #5 - Test Yourself

Everyone knows that time is money. There is no need to spend too much of your time or too little of your time preparing for the test. You should only spend as much of your precious time preparing as is necessary for you to get the score you need.

Once you have taken a practice test under real conditions of time constraints, then you will know if you are ready for the test or not.

If you have scored extremely high the first time that you take the practice test, then there is not much point in spending countless hours studying. You are already there.

Benchmark your abilities by retaking practice tests and seeing how much you have improved. Once you score high enough to guarantee success, then you are ready.

If you have scored well below where you need, then knuckle down and begin studying in earnest. Check your improvement regularly through the use of practice tests under real conditions. Above all, don't worry, panic, or give up. The key is perseverance!

Then, when you go to take the test, remain confident and remember how well you did on the practice tests. If you can score high enough on a practice test, then you can do the same on the real thing.

Top 20 Test Taking Tips

1. Carefully follow all the test registration procedures
2. Know the test directions, duration, topics, question types, how many questions
3. Setup a flexible study schedule at least 3-4 weeks before test day
4. Study during the time of day you are most alert, relaxed, and stress free
5. Maximize your learning style; visual learner use visual study aids, auditory learner use auditory study aids
6. Focus on your weakest knowledge base
7. Find a study partner to review with and help clarify questions
8. Practice, practice, practice
9. Get a good night's sleep; don't try to cram the night before the test
10. Eat a well balanced meal
11. Know the exact physical location of the testing site; drive the route to the site prior to test day
12. Bring a set of ear plugs; the testing center could be noisy
13. Wear comfortable, loose fitting, layered clothing to the testing center; prepare for it to be either cold or hot during the test
14. Bring at least 2 current forms of ID to the testing center
15. Arrive to the test early; be prepared to wait and be patient
16. Eliminate the obviously wrong answer choices, then guess the first remaining choice
17. Pace yourself; don't rush, but keep working and move on if you get stuck
18. Maintain a positive attitude even if the test is going poorly
19. Keep your first answer unless you are positive it is wrong
20. Check your work, don't make a careless mistake

General Strategies

The most important thing you can do is to ignore your fears and jump into the test immediately- do not be overwhelmed by any strange-sounding terms. You have to jump into the test like jumping into a pool- all at once is the easiest way.

Make Predictions
As you read and understand the question, try to guess what the answer will be. Remember that several of the answer choices are wrong, and once you begin reading them, your mind will immediately become cluttered with answer choices designed to throw you off. Your mind is typically the most focused immediately after you have read the question and digested its contents. If you can, try to predict what the correct answer will be. You may be surprised at what you can predict.

Quickly scan the choices and see if your prediction is in the listed answer choices. If it is, then you can be quite confident that you have the right answer. It still won't hurt to check the other answer choices, but most of the time, you've got it!

Answer the Question
It may seem obvious to only pick answer choices that answer the question, but the test writers can create some excellent answer choices that are wrong. Don't pick an answer just because it sounds right, or you believe it to be true. It MUST answer the question. Once you've made your selection, always go back and check it against the question and make sure that you didn't misread the question, and the answer choice does answer the question posed.

Benchmark
After you read the first answer choice, decide if you think it sounds correct or not. If it doesn't, move on to the next answer choice. If it does, mentally mark that answer choice. This doesn't mean that you've definitely selected it as your answer choice, it just means that it's the best you've seen thus far. Go ahead and read the next choice. If the next choice is worse than the one you've already selected, keep going to the next answer choice. If the next choice is better than the choice you've already selected, mentally mark the new answer choice as your best guess.

The first answer choice that you select becomes your standard. Every other answer choice must be benchmarked against that standard. That choice is correct until proven otherwise by another answer choice beating it out. Once you've decided that no other answer choice seems as good, do one final check to ensure that your answer choice answers the question posed.

Valid Information
Don't discount any of the information provided in the question. Every piece of information may be necessary to determine the correct answer. None of the information in the question is there to throw you off (while the answer choices will certainly have information to throw you off). If two seemingly unrelated topics are discussed, don't ignore either. You can be confident there is a relationship, or it wouldn't be included in the question, and you are probably going to have to determine what is that relationship to find the answer.

Avoid "Fact Traps"
Don't get distracted by a choice that is factually true. Your search is for the answer that answers the question. Stay focused and don't fall for an answer that is true but incorrect. Always go back to the question and make sure you're choosing an answer that actually answers the question and is not just a true statement. An answer can be factually correct, but it MUST answer the question asked. Additionally, two answers can both be seemingly correct, so be sure to read all of the answer choices, and make

sure that you get the one that BEST answers the question.

Milk the Question
Some of the questions may throw you completely off. They might deal with a subject you have not been exposed to, or one that you haven't reviewed in years. While your lack of knowledge about the subject will be a hindrance, the question itself can give you many clues that will help you find the correct answer. Read the question carefully and look for clues. Watch particularly for adjectives and nouns describing difficult terms or words that you don't recognize. Regardless of if you completely understand a word or not, replacing it with a synonym either provided or one you more familiar with may help you to understand what the questions are asking. Rather than wracking your mind about specific detailed information concerning a difficult term or word, try to use mental substitutes that are easier to understand.

The Trap of Familiarity
Don't just choose a word because you recognize it. On difficult questions, you may not recognize a number of words in the answer choices. The test writers don't put "make-believe" words on the test; so don't think that just because you only recognize all the words in one answer choice means that answer choice must be correct. If you only recognize words in one answer choice, then focus on that one. Is it correct? Try your best to determine if it is correct. If it is, that is great, but if it doesn't, eliminate it. Each word and answer choice you eliminate increases your chances of getting the question correct, even if you then have to guess among the unfamiliar choices.

Eliminate Answers
Eliminate choices as soon as you realize they are wrong. But be careful! Make sure you consider all of the possible answer choices. Just because one appears right, doesn't mean that the next one won't be even better!

The test writers will usually put more than one good answer choice for every question, so read all of them. Don't worry if you are stuck between two that seem right. By getting down to just two remaining possible choices, your odds are now 50/50. Rather than wasting too much time, play the odds. You are guessing, but guessing wisely, because you've been able to knock out some of the answer choices that you know are wrong. If you are eliminating choices and realize that the last answer choice you are left with is also obviously wrong, don't panic. Start over and consider each choice again. There may easily be something that you missed the first time and will realize on the second pass.

Tough Questions
If you are stumped on a problem or it appears too hard or too difficult, don't waste time. Move on! Remember though, if you can quickly check for obviously incorrect answer choices, your chances of guessing correctly are greatly improved. Before you completely give up, at least try to knock out a couple of possible answers. Eliminate what you can and then guess at the remaining answer choices before moving on.

Brainstorm
If you get stuck on a difficult question, spend a few seconds quickly brainstorming. Run through the complete list of possible answer choices. Look at each choice and ask yourself, "Could this answer the question satisfactorily?" Go through each answer choice and consider it independently of the other. By systematically going through all possibilities, you may find something that you would otherwise overlook. Remember that when you get stuck, it's important to try to keep moving.

Read Carefully
Understand the problem. Read the question and answer choices carefully. Don't miss the question because you misread the terms. You have plenty of time to read each question thoroughly and make sure you

- 12 -

understand what is being asked. Yet a happy medium must be attained, so don't waste too much time. You must read carefully, but efficiently.

Face Value

When in doubt, use common sense. Always accept the situation in the problem at face value. Don't read too much into it. These problems will not require you to make huge leaps of logic. The test writers aren't trying to throw you off with a cheap trick. If you have to go beyond creativity and make a leap of logic in order to have an answer choice answer the question, then you should look at the other answer choices. Don't overcomplicate the problem by creating theoretical relationships or explanations that will warp time or space. These are normal problems rooted in reality. It's just that the applicable relationship or explanation may not be readily apparent and you have to figure things out. Use your common sense to interpret anything that isn't clear.

Prefixes

If you're having trouble with a word in the question or answer choices, try dissecting it. Take advantage of every clue that the word might include. Prefixes and suffixes can be a huge help. Usually they allow you to determine a basic meaning. Pre- means before, post- means after, pro - is positive, de- is negative. From these prefixes and suffixes, you can get an idea of the general meaning of the word and try to put it into context. Beware though of any traps. Just because con is the opposite of pro, doesn't necessarily mean congress is the opposite of progress!

Hedge Phrases

Watch out for critical "hedge" phrases, such as likely, may, can, will often, sometimes, often, almost, mostly, usually, generally, rarely, sometimes. Question writers insert these hedge phrases to cover every possibility. Often an answer choice will be wrong simply because it leaves no room for exception. Avoid answer choices that have definitive words like "exactly," and "always".

Switchback Words

Stay alert for "switchbacks". These are the words and phrases frequently used to alert you to shifts in thought. The most common switchback word is "but". Others include although, however, nevertheless, on the other hand, even though, while, in spite of, despite, regardless of.

New Information

Correct answer choices will rarely have completely new information included. Answer choices typically are straightforward reflections of the material asked about and will directly relate to the question. If a new piece of information is included in an answer choice that doesn't even seem to relate to the topic being asked about, then that answer choice is likely incorrect. All of the information needed to answer the question is usually provided for you, and so you should not have to make guesses that are unsupported or choose answer choices that require unknown information that cannot be reasoned on its own.

Time Management

On technical questions, don't get lost on the technical terms. Don't spend too much time on any one question. If you don't know what a term means, then since you don't have a dictionary, odds are you aren't going to get much further. You should immediately recognize terms as whether or not you know them. If you don't, work with the other clues that you have, the other answer choices and terms provided, but don't waste too much time trying to figure out a difficult term.

Contextual Clues

Look for contextual clues. An answer can be right but not correct. The contextual clues will help you find the answer that is most right and is correct. Understand the context in which a phrase or statement is made.

This will help you make important distinctions.

Don't Panic

Panicking will not answer any questions for you. Therefore, it isn't helpful. When you first see the question, if your mind goes blank, take a deep breath. Force yourself to mechanically go through the steps of solving the problem and using the strategies you've learned.

Pace Yourself

Don't get clock fever. It's easy to be overwhelmed when you're looking at a page full of questions, your mind is full of random thoughts and feeling confused, and the clock is ticking down faster than you would like. Calm down and maintain the pace that you have set for yourself. As long as you are on track by monitoring your pace, you are guaranteed to have enough time for yourself. When you get to the last few minutes of the test, it may seem like you won't have enough time left, but if you only have as many questions as you should have left at that point, then you're right on track!

Answer Selection

The best way to pick an answer choice is to eliminate all of those that are wrong, until only one is left and confirm that is the correct answer. Sometimes though, an answer choice may immediately look right. Be careful! Take a second to make sure that the other choices are not equally obvious. Don't make a hasty mistake. There are only two times that you should stop before checking other answers. First is when you are positive that the answer choice you have selected is correct. Second is when time is almost out and you have to make a quick guess!

Check Your Work

Since you will probably not know every term listed and the answer to every question, it is important that you get credit for the ones that you do know. Don't miss any questions through careless mistakes. If at all possible, try to take a second to look back over your answer selection and make sure you've selected the correct answer choice and haven't made a costly careless mistake (such as marking an answer choice that you didn't mean to mark). This quick double check should more than pay for itself in caught mistakes for the time it costs.

Beware of Directly Quoted Answers

Sometimes an answer choice will repeat word for word a portion of the question or reference section. However, beware of such exact duplication – it may be a trap! More than likely, the correct choice will paraphrase or summarize a point, rather than being exactly the same wording.

Slang

Scientific sounding answers are better than slang ones. An answer choice that begins "To compare the outcomes…" is much more likely to be correct than one that begins "Because some people insisted…"

Extreme Statements

Avoid wild answers that throw out highly controversial ideas that are proclaimed as established fact. An answer choice that states the "process should used in certain situations, if…" is much more likely to be correct than one that states the "process should be discontinued completely." The first is a calm rational statement and doesn't even make a definitive, uncompromising stance, using a hedge word "if" to provide wiggle room, whereas the second choice is a radical idea and far more extreme.

Answer Choice Families

When you have two or more answer choices that are direct opposites or parallels, one of them is usually the correct answer. For instance, if one answer choice states "x increases" and another answer choice states "x decreases" or "y increases," then those two or three answer choices are very similar in construction and fall into the same family of answer choices. A family of answer choices is when two or three answer choices are very similar in construction, and yet often have a directly opposite meaning. Usually the correct answer choice will be in that family of answer choices. The "odd man out" or answer choice that doesn't seem to fit the parallel construction of the other answer choices is more likely to be incorrect.

Registering for the NSCA-CPT Licensure Test

Registering Link:
http://www.nsca-cc.org/exam_info/how_to_register_nsca_cpt.html

NSCA Certification Commission
http://www.nsca-cc.org/

Test Schedule
http://www.nsca-cc.org/exam_info/nsca_cpt_schedule.html

Contact Information:

NSCA Certification Commission
3333 Landmark Circle • Lincoln, NE 68504
Phone: 402.476.6669 • Toll-Free: 888.746.2378
Fax: 402.476.7141 • Fax On Demand: 877.441.2378
E-Mail: commission@nsca-cc.org

NSCA-CPT Content

<table>
<tr><th colspan="2">NSCA-Certified Personal Trainer® Examination
Content Distribution</th></tr>
<tr><th>DOMAIN</th><th>No. of questions</th></tr>
<tr><td>Client Consultation/Assessment</td><td>28</td></tr>
<tr><td>Program Planning</td><td>49</td></tr>
<tr><td>Techniques of Exercise</td><td>49</td></tr>
<tr><td>Safety, Emergency Procedures, and Legal Issues</td><td>14</td></tr>
<tr><td>**Total**</td><td>140</td></tr>
<tr><td>Number of video questions (already included in the total)</td><td>35</td></tr>
<tr><td>**Exam length**</td><td>3 hours</td></tr>
</table>

NSCA-CPT Testing Cost

The costs for the NSCA-CPT Examination are:

	Early Registration	Registration Cut-off
NSCA Member		
Initial Registration	$225	$260
Retake Fee	$180	$205
Nonmember		
Initial Registration	$330	$365
Retake Fee	$285	$310

VOCABULARY: Exercise Terminology

Abduction refers to the movement of a body part away from the midline of the body.

Absolute refers to just the actual weight of body fat even though your body is composed of both muscle and fat.

Adduction refers to movement of a body part toward the midline of the body.

Aerobic refers to conditions or processes that occur in the presence of, or requiring oxygen.

Aerobic capacity is the total amount of work that can be performed by the aerobic energy system.

Aerobic fitness is the ability to perform prolonged periods of work without getting tired. During aerobic exercise, you should be able to carry on a conversation.

Ambient heart rate is your heart rate during the day when you aren't really doing anything, but it's not truly resting either. Take it at the same time, in the same circumstances, daily.

Amino acids refer to the building blocks of protein.

Anaerobic exercise is an exercise done for a short period of time usually 1 to 2 minutes, develops speed, but does not develop overall fitness

Antioxidants refer to specific vitamins, minerals, and nutrients that protect the body against free radicals.

Basal metabolic rate or BMR refers to the rate at which the body burns calories over a 24-hour period, while at complete rest.

Blood pressure refers to the pressure within the arterial system caused by blood flow.

Body composition refers to the make up of lean and fat tissue in the body.

Body fat percentage refers to the percentage of fat in the body.

Body mass index or BMI refers to the numerical equivalent of over or underweight, derived from an equation utilizing body weight and height.

Buff refers to a large and muscular body. The term is usually directed towards the male gender. A female would be "Buffy".

Calisthenics refers to exercises that use the body weight as resistance. Push-ups and crunches are examples.

Calorie refers to a measure of the energy value of food.

Carbohydrates refer to one of the six nutrients used by the body for energy. Dietary sources of carbohydrates include sugars, grains, rice, potatoes and beans. 1 gram=4 calories

Cardio is a shortened form normally known as cardiovascular training or aerobic conditioning.

Cardiorespiratory fitness is a health-related component of physical fitness that relates to the ability of the circulatory and respiratory systems to supply oxygen during sustained physical activity.

Cardiovascular is a term that refers to the heart and blood vessels.

Carotid pulse is a pulse located on the carotid artery that is located down from the corner of the eye, just under the jawbone.

Cellulite refers to the subcutaneous fat, commonly found in the thighs and butt and usually appears dimpled.

Cellulose is a type of carbohydrate that is composed of glucose sugars.

Cholesterol refers to the lipids found only in animal products and produced by the body.

Circuit training refers to a training technique that involves moving from one exercise to another usually 10 to 12. Each exercise works a different muscle group until each muscle has been worked.

Cool down refers to the part of an exercise program that follows the workout and reduces the heart rate.

Crunches are exercises that isolate the abs without stress on the lower back. Crunches are preferred over sit-ups.

Dehydration refers to the loss of fluids from the body to below normal levels.

Diuretic refers to any agent that increases the flow of urine.

Dynamic stretching involves stretching movements performed at gradually increased speed.

Ectomorph refers to a body type that is characterized by a light build and slight muscular development.

Electrolytes refer to minerals such as chloride, sodium, potassium, calcium, and magnesium.

Empty calorie is a term used to indicate food-contributing calories with little food value and nutrients. Examples are alcohol and simple sugars.

Endomorph refers to a body type that is characterized by a stocky build, wide hips, and heavy fat storage.

Endorphins are substances in the brain that induce "runner's high" or good feelings during prolonged exercise.

Endurance is the ability to maintain a physical activity over time.

Energy balance refers to the relationship between energy intake (input of food) and energy output (energy expenditure).

Energy expenditure is the energy cost to the body of physical activity, usually measured in kilocalories.

Exercise is defined as planned, structured, and repetitive bodily movement done to improve or maintain one or more components of physical fitness.

Extension refers to the straightening of a body part away from the body. An example is straightening the elbow.

Fat is an essential nutrient that provides energy, energy storage and insulation to the body.

FITT is a theory governing proper frequency, intensity, time and type of exercise.

Flexibility refers to the ability to flex and extend the body's joints through their full range of motion.

Free radicals refer to highly reactive molecules that are known to damage muscle fibers, causes inflammation and fatigue and the suppression of the immune system.

Frequency refers to the number of times.

Functional living is the ability to successfully and to safely perform activities related to a daily routine with sufficient energy, strength/endurance, flexibility, and coordination.

Glucose refers to a simple sugar; the form in which all carbs (carbohydrates) are used as the body's principle energy source.

HDL is the abbreviation for high-density lipoproteins, the "good" cholesterol that returns unused fat to the liver for disposal.

High impact aerobics are exercises in which both feet leave the ground simultaneously.

Hyperextension refers to the extension of the angle between bones of a joint to a greater degree than normal.

Hypertrophy refers to an increase in muscle size.

Insulin refers to the hormone that is essential for the correct maintenance level and metabolism of blood sugar.

Intensity refers to the rate of performing work.

Interval training refers to measured periods of exercise followed by measured periods of rest.

Isometric action refers to the contraction of a muscle without significant movement; also referred to as static tension

Isotonic contraction refers to the alternate contraction and relaxation of large muscles against a natural resistance.

LDL is an abbreviation for low-density lipoprotein also known as the "bad" cholesterol.

Kegel exercises are exercises to strengthen the muscles of the pelvic floor which leads to more control and prevents urine leakage.

Lean body mass refers to all body tissue except stored fat. It includes water, muscle, bones, and other body organs such as the heart, liver and kidneys.

Low-impact aerobics is a type of exercise in which one foot always stays in contact with the floor.

Lumbar refers to the area of the spine or back between the ribs and pelvis.

Maximum heart rate is the fastest and hardest your heart muscle can beat without being able to beat any faster.

Metabolism refers to all of the chemical processes that are taking place in your body to transfer food and other substances into energy and waste.

Minerals are essential dietary nutrients that are responsible for a number of biological functions such as muscle growth, fat metabolism, and good health.

Moderate physical activity is any activity that makes the breathing slightly harder than normal and the person feel warmer but without perspiring.

Monounsaturated fat is a type of fatty acid that can lower blood cholesterol levels.

Obese refers to having a BMI of 30 or greater or more than 25% body fat in males or 32% body fat in females.

Physical activity is defined as bodily movement that is produced by the contraction of skeletal muscle that substantially increases energy expenditure.

Physical fitness is a set of attributes that people have or achieve that relate to the ability to perform physical activity. The components of physical fitness include body composition, cardiovascular fitness, flexibility, and muscular strength and endurance.

Polyunsaturated fat refers to the type of fatty acid that can lower blood cholesterol levels.

Power refers to the quick movement of the body and strength for the performance of activities.

Prone refers to lying in the face down position.

Protein refers to one of the body's nutrients that builds and repairs tissues.

Sedentary describes a person who is relatively inactive and has a lifestyle characterized by a lot of sitting.

Range of motion refers to the complete movement of a joint.

Reciprocal movement refers to movement in the opposite direction

Recovery time refers to the time it takes for the heart rate to recover to pre-exercise rate.

Rep (repetition) refers to one repetition or complete movement of an exercise.
Resistance training refers to the use of weights to build lean muscle tissue.

Resting heart rate refers to the number of heartbeats per minute after sitting quietly for 15-20 minutes.

Saturated fat refers to the fatty acid that increases blood cholesterol.

Set is a term that refers to a fixed number of repetitions.

Shin splint is a term that applies to any pain in the front portion of the lower leg.

Sprain refers to an injury that damages ligaments as well as joints.

Spot reducing refers to a false assumption that an individual can "burn" fat only in desired areas.

Static stretches are slow, controlled stretching through a joint's full range of motion.

Strain refers to muscle pull, a stretch, tear or rip of the muscle or adjacent connective tissue.

Strength refers to the amount of force a muscle or muscle group can exert against resistance.

Strength training refers to applying a greater load than normal to a muscle to increase its capability.

Supine refers to lying in a face up position.

Supplements refer to the concentrated forms of nutritional components, such as minerals, vitamins, and amino acids that an individual takes to enhance the nutritional value of food.

Target heart rate is a number range that is your target for workouts because of your fitness, health, or performance goals.

Vigorous physical activity is any activity which makes the heart beat rapidly and breathing fairly hard (but not breathless), and may make the individual perspire.
Typical activities that would require vigorous activity include running, jogging, swimming, hard cycling, basketball and football.

Vitamins are organic food substances present in animals and plants. They are essential for cell building and the operation of bodily functions.

Warm-ups are preliminary activities that an individual does to prepare the body for more vigorous exercise. Warm-ups should consist of light, progressive activities that stimulate the muscles, heart and lungs.

Water intake refers to the amount of water needed by the body to stay hydrated. The general formula for minimum recommended water intake is as follows.
Body weight in lb. x 0.5 oz

BODY COMPOSITION

Body composition

Assessing clients' body composition helps set exercise goals and establish a baseline for measuring progress. Skinfold calipers can be used to estimate body fat percentage by summing the values from three (9) or four body sites (10) and using a skinfold equation to compare this sum with a table of norms. For men, 25% or more body fat elevates the risk for health problems such as adult-onset diabetes, cardiovascular disease, and hypertension; for women, 38% or more body fat presents an elevated risk. Bioelectrical impedance devices are useful for in-office evaluation of body composition if patients are adequately hydrated.

BMI

The term BMI is often used when discussing the obesity epidemic, but what is BMI?

BMI stands for **B**ody **M**ass **I**ndex. It is a number that shows body weight adjusted for height. BMI can be calculated with simple math using inches and pounds, or meters and kilograms. For adults aged 20 years or older, BMI falls into one of these categories: underweight, normal, overweight, or obese.

What is BMI?

BMI	Weight Status
Below 18.5	Underweight
18.5 - 24.9	Normal
25.0 - 29.9	Overweight
30.0 and Above	Obese

BMI *correlates* with body fat. The relation between fatness and BMI differs with age and gender. For example, women are more likely to have a higher percent of body fat than men for the same BMI. On average, older people may have more body fat than younger adults with the same BMI.

How does BMI relate to health?

The BMI ranges are based on the effect body weight has on disease and death. As BMI increases, the risk for some disease increases. Some common conditions related to overweight and obesity include:

- Premature death
- Cardiovascular disease
- High blood pressure
- Osteoarthritis
- Some cancers
- Diabetes

BMI is only one of many factors used to predict risk for disease. BMI cannot be used to tell a person if he/she has a disease such as diabetes or cancer. It is important to remember that weight is only one factor that is related to disease.

Now, use the following table to see how healthy the BMI figure is:

Men	Women	Risk Factor
<20.7	<19.1	Underweight. The lower the BMI the greater the risk
20.7 to 26.4	19.1 to 25.8	Normal, very low risk
26.4 to 27.8	25.8 to 27.3	Marginally overweight, some risk
27.8 to 31.1	27.3 to 32.2	Overweight, moderate risk
31.1 to 45.4	32.3 to 44.8	Severe overweight, high risk
>45.4	>44.8	Morbid obesity, very high risk

You can calculate BMI using either feet, inches, and pounds, or meters, centimeters, and kilograms.

English Formula

Body Mass Index can be calculated using pounds and inches with this equation

$$BMI = \left(\frac{\text{Weight in Pounds}}{(\text{Height in inches}) \times (\text{Height in inches})} \right) \times 703$$

For example, a person who weighs 220 pounds and is 6 feet 3 inches tall has a BMI of 27.5.

$$\left(\frac{220 \text{ lbs.}}{(75 \text{ inches}) \times (75 \text{ inches})} \right) \times 703 = 27.5$$

Metric Formula

Body Mass Index can also be calculated using kilograms and meters (or centimeters).

$$BMI = \frac{\text{Weight in Kilograms}}{(\text{Height in Meters}) \times (\text{Height in Meters})}$$

or

$$BMI = \left(\frac{\text{Weight in Kilograms}}{(\text{Height in centimeters}) \times (\text{Height in centimeters})} \right) \times 10{,}000$$

For example, a person who weighs 99.79 Kilograms and is 1.905 Meters (190.50 centimeters) tall has a BMI of 27.5.

$$\frac{99.79 \text{ Kg}}{(1.905 \text{ m}) \times (1.905 \text{ m})} = 27.5$$

MALES vs. FEMALES

Key Facts:

The "typical" young untrained male will have an absolute VO2 max of 3.5 liters/min, while the typical same-age female will be about 2 liters/min.

If you compare average bodyfat in males and females, you will find that young untrained women average about 25% bodyfat compared to 15% in young men.

Women who are physically active are likely to be more at risk of iron deficiency.

Females in general have a lower maximum aerobic power capacity than men (65-75% of male aerobic power) due to lower haemoglobin levels and a greater amount of adipose tissue (fat).

On average females have a lower blood hemoglobin content than males, up to 10% lower.

There is some evidence, that the female heart is slightly smaller relative to body size than the male heart.

Female skeletal muscle is not distinguishable from male skeletal muscle.

The fiber type distribution (percentage of slow versus fast fibers) is not different in the male and female population.

Male and female skeletal muscle responds similarly to endurance exercise.

Situations like running or cycling, may actually favor females in general, due to narrower upper bodies for a given total body mass, and potentially less wind or water drag.

There is no gender difference in the ability of men and women to burn fat.

Men have an advantage in evaporative cooling, but women have an advantage in radiant cooling.

It appears that the strength and power differences between the sexes are a function of muscle quantity only.

Evidence shows that women players suffer more anterior cruciate knee ligament damage than males in certain sports.

Respiratory Review

The respiratory stem includes the nose, nasal cavity, sinuses, pharynx, larynx, trachea, bronchial tree, and lungs. Air enters the nose, travels through the nasal cavity where the air is warmed. The air goes through the pharynx, which functions as a common duct for air and food. Then the larynx, which is at the top of the trachea and holds the vocal cords allows passage of air. The trachea divides into the right and left bronchi on the way into the bronchial tree and the lungs. The right lung has three lobes and the left lung has two lobes. Gas exchange occurs between the air and the blood within the alveoli, which are tiny air sacs. Diffusion is the mechanism by which oxygen and carbon dioxide are exchanged.

Breathing is controlled by the medulla oblongata and pons. Inspiration is controlled by changes in the thoracic cavity. Air fills the lung because of atmospheric pressure pushing air in. Expansion of the lungs is aided by surface tension, which holds pleural membranes together. In addition, the diaphragm, which is located just below the lungs, and stimulated by phrenic nerve acts as a suction pump to encourage inspiration. Expiration comes from the recoil of tissues and the surface tension of the alveoli.

Aerobic respiration occurs in the presence of oxygen and mostly takes place in the mitochondria of a cell. Anaerobic respiration occurs in the absence of oxygen and takes place in the cytoplasm of a cell. Both of these mechanisms occur in cellular respiration in humans. With anaerobic respiration glucose is broken down and produces less ATP when compared to aerobic respiration.

Anoxia- absence of oxygen in tissue
Atelectasis- collapse of a lung
Dyspnea- difficulty in the breathing cycle
Hypercapnia- excessive carbon dioxide in the blood
Tidal Volume-amount of air that normally moves in and out of the lungs

MINUTE VENTILATION, RESIDUAL LUNG VOLUME, FORCED VITAL CAPACITY, TOTAL LUNG CAPACITY; VALSALVA MANEUVER:

Minute ventilation is the volume of air inhaled and exhaled into and out of the lungs in one minute. **Residual lung volume** is air that always stays in the lungs to keep the lungs from collapsing even after the person breathes out all the air he or she can. **Forced vital capacity** is the amount of air that a person can force out of his or her lungs after breathing in very deeply. **Total lung capacity** is the total volume of air the lungs can hold, found by adding residual lung volume to forced vital capacity. The **Valsalva maneuver** is holding one's breath when doing a difficult exercise. The epiglottis stops air to the windpipe, which increases pressure in the lungs and may disrupt the flow of blood back to the heart and brain. Dizziness or fainting may result, but some people may experience a dangerously irregular heartbeat.

ENERGY PRODUCTION

ATP—ITS ROLE IN THE BODY; METABOLIC PATHWAYS

ATP is adenosine triphosphate, the molecule in which fuel is generated/stored in the body. ATP requires energy to be made from ADP (adenosine diphosphate) and a phosphate molecule. It then can release energy when the phosphate molecule is broken off of the ATP. The energy created by the breakup of ATP is then available for the body to use in activity or basic functions. This energy can be made via anaerobic methods (without oxygen) or via aerobic method (with oxygen). The energy to create ATP is made from three different systems (also called metabolic pathways), the anaerobic phosphagen system, the anaerobic glycolytic system (or lactic acid system), and the aerobic (oxidative) system.

ATP PRODUCTION—TWO ANAEROBIC SYSTEMS:

The **anaerobic phosphagen system** (ATP-PC) is used for fast energy. Creatine phosphate (CP), also called phosphocreatine (PC) breaks into creatine and phosphorus by the addition of an enzyme, creatine kinase (CK). The resulting energy then creates ATP from ADP and phosphate. Once creatine phosphate is depleted in the body (within 15-20 seconds), this system will no longer provide the needed energy. The **anaerobic glycolytic** (lactic acid) system uses glucose to create ATP. Once creatine phosphate is depleted, the enzyme phosphofructokinase (PFK) will break glucose down into pyruvic acid, a process that releases ATP. If insufficient oxygen is present, the pyruvic acid turns into lactic acid, which builds up and creates exhaustion and difficulty breathing, signaling the body to reduce activity.

ATP PRODUCTION—AEROBIC SYSTEM:

The aerobic system is the most common system of ATP production, meeting most of the body's needs. Energy is formed in the presence of oxygen. First, aerobic glycolysis converts glucose (from carbohydrates) into pyruvic acid. The pyruvic acid turns into acetyl CoA inside the mitochondria of the cells and enters the Krebs Cycle. Meanwhile, fats broken into free fatty acids (FFA) and proteins reduced to amino acids are converted into acetyl CoA. Second is the Krebs Cycle, resulting in the removal of hydrogen ions and carbon molecules. Carbon combines with oxygen to form CO_2 and is breathed out, and the hydrogen enters the electron transport system. The flow of hydrogen electrons makes energy for a large quantity of ATP. This system makes much more ATP than anaerobic systems, but needs help from anaerobic systems when oxygen is depleted or energy is needed fast.

ANAEROBIC THRESHOLD, MAXIMAL OXYGEN UPTAKE and EPOC:

The **anaerobic or lactate threshold** is the instant when the body must switch from forming energy though the aerobic system and must begin to use the anaerobic pathways to create energy. Lactic acid will then begin to build up in the cells. This threshold will increase as the person becomes more fit.

Maximal oxygen uptake (or VO2 max) is the most oxygen a person uses when he or she is exercising as hard as possible. This presumably measures the ability of the body to make ATP through the aerobic system. As a person becomes more fit, he or she will be able to take in and use more oxygen and thus make more ATP aerobically. **EPOC** is excess post-exercise oxygen consumption is how much oxygen is breathed in just after a strenuous activity is finished. All three of these indicators are measures of aerobic fitness.

DETERMINING EXERCISE INTENSITY

HEART RATE METHODS:

Estimate the highest rate the heart will beat by subtracting the person's age from 220. Multiply the percentage of the maximum heart rate you would like to reach by the result to obtain the target heart rate. The Karvonen formula (or HRR method) uses the estimated maximum heart rate but also uses resting heart rate and is thus considered more accurate.
- Find estimated maximum heart rate (220 – age)
- Subtract the heart rate at rest from the estimated maximum heart rate to get HRR
- Multiply HRR by the intensity (expressed as a percentage of the maximum heart rate) to get the percent of HRR
- Add the percent of HRR to the resting heart rate and the result is the target heart rate. Target heart rate range is usually expressed as a range, so calculate both the lower and upper targets.

RATE OF PERCEIVED EXERTION METHOD:

Rate of perceived exertion is a subjective form of measuring intensity. The subject rates his/her own exertion as they interpret it. The original RPE scale (also called the Borg scale) was based on a range between 6 and 20, while the newer, revised scale rates intensity on a scale of 0 to 10. Clients must be taught how to relate their perceived exertion to the scale. The original scale determined that exercise between 12-16 (on a 20-point scale) of intensity was the target, characterized as somewhat hard to hard. The revised 10-point scale promotes a target of 2.5-5, characterized by moderate to strong intensity.

METS METHOD:

A MET ("metabolic equivalent") is a way to measure how much energy is used. One MET is the rate at which the average person uses oxygen when not exerting himself (per pound of body weight). By using multiples of METS, one can calculate the approximate amount of oxygen used during the activity, and thus presume the amount of energy being used. One MET is 3.5ml of oxygen per kilogram of body weight per minute. Scientists have identified the MET levels of various familiar activities, which can be obtained in a chart. In order to improve cardiorespiratory fitness, MET levels must be increased as fitness improves. Clients should choose more intense activities—listed as utilizing more METS.

One MET is defined as the energy it takes to sit quietly. For the average adult, this is about one calorie per every 2.2 pounds of body weight per hour someone who weighs 160 pounds would burn approximately 70 calories an hour while sitting or sleeping.

MET Levels and Daily Activities	
	METs
Mild	
Playing the piano	2.3
Golf (with cart)	2.5
Dancing (ballroom)	2.9
Moderate	
Walking (3 mph)	3.3
Cycling (leisurely)	3.5
Calisthenics	4
Golf (no cart)	4.4
Walking	4.5
Vigorous	
Chopping wood	4.9
Tennis (doubles)	5
Cycling	5.7
Skiing (water or downhill)	6.8
Climbing hills (no load)	6.9
Swimming	7
Walking (5 mph)	8
Rope skipping	12
Squash	12.1
Activities of daily living	
Lying quietly	1
Sitting; light activity	1.5
Walking from house to car or bus	2.5
Taking out trash	3
Walking the dog	3
Household tasks, moderate effort	3.5
Lifting items continuously	4
Raking lawn	4
Gardening (no lifting)	4.4
Mowing lawn (power mower)	4.5

CIRCULATORY SYSTEM

Functions

The circulatory system serves:
1. to conduct nutrients and oxygen to the tissues;

- 28 -

2. to remove waste materials by transporting nitrogenous compounds to the kidneys and carbon dioxide to the lungs;
3. to transport chemical messengers (hormones) to target organs and modulate and integrate the internal milieu of the body;
4. to transport agents which serve the body in allergic, immune, and infectious responses;
5. to initiate clotting and thereby prevent blood loss;
6. to maintain body temperature;
7. to produce, carry and contain blood;
8. to transfer body reserves, specifically mineral salts, to areas of need.

General Components and Structure

The circulatory system consists of the heart, blood vessels, blood and lymphatics. It is a network of tubular structures through which blood travels to and from all the parts of the body. In vertebrates this is a completely closed circuit system, as William Harvey (1628) once demonstrated. The heart is a modified, specialized, powerful pumping blood vessel. Arteries, eventually becoming arterioles, conduct blood to capillaries (essentially endothelial tubes), and venules, eventually becoming veins, return blood from the capillary bed to the heart.

COURSE OF CIRCULATION

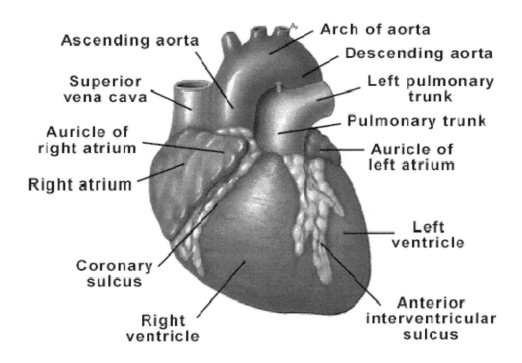

Systemic Route:

a. *Arterial system.* Blood is delivered by the pulmonary veins (two from each lung) to the left atrium, passes through the bicuspid (mitral) valve into the left ventricle and then is pumped into the ascending aorta; backflow here is prevented by the aortic semilunar valves. The aortic arch toward the right side gives rise to the brachiocephalic (innominate) artery which divides into the right subclavian and right common carotid arteries. Next, arising from the arch is the common carotid artery, then the left subclavian artery.

The subclavians supply the upper limbs. As the subclavian arteries leave the axilla (armpit) and enter the arm (brachium), they are called brachial arteries. Below the elbow these main trunk lines divide into ulnar and radial arteries, which supply the forearm and eventually form a set of arterial arches in the hand which give rise to common and proper digital arteries. The descending (dorsal) aorta continues along the posterior aspect of the thorax giving rise to the segmental intercostals arteries. After passage "through" (behind) the diaphragm it is called the abdominal aorta.

At the pelvic rim the abdominal aorta divides into the right and left common iliac arteries. These divide into the internal iliacs, which supply the pelvic organs, and the external iliacs, which supply the lower limb.

b. *Venous system.* Veins are frequently multiple and variations are common. They return blood originating in the capillaries of peripheral and distal body parts to the heart.

Hepatic Portal System: Blood draining the alimentary tract (intestines), pancreas, spleen and gall bladder does not return directly to the systemic circulation, but is relayed by the hepatic portal system of veins to and through the liver. In the liver, absorbed foodstuffs and wastes are processed. After processing, the liver returns the blood via hepatic veins to the inferior vena cava and from there to the heart.

Pulmonary Circuit: Blood is oxygenated and depleted of metabolic products such as carbon dioxide in the lungs.

Lymphatic Drainage: A network of lymphatic capillaries permeates the body tissues. Lymph is a fluid similar in composition to blood plasma, and tissue fluids not reabsorbed into blood capillaries are transported via the lymphatic system eventually to join the venous system at the junction of the left internal jugular and subclavian veins.

The Heart

The heart is a highly specialized blood vessel which pumps 72 times per minute and propels about 4,000 gallons (about 15,000 liters) of blood daily to the tissues. It is composed of:
>   Endocardium (lining coat; epithelium)
>   Myocardium (middle coat; cardiac muscle)
>   Epicardium (external coat or visceral layer of pericardium; epithelium and mostly connective tissue)
>   Impulse conducting system

Cardiac Nerves: Modification of the intrinsic rhythmicity of the heart muscle is produced by cardiac nerves of the sympathetic and parasympathetic nervous system. Stimulation of the sympathetic system increases the rate and force of the heartbeat and dilates the coronary arteries. Stimulation of the parasympathetic (vagus nerve) reduces the rate and force of the heartbeat and constricts the coronary circulation. Visceral afferent (sensory) fibers from the heart end almost wholly in the first four segments of the thoracic spinal cord.

Cardiac Cycle: Alternating contraction and relaxation is repeated about 75 times per minute; the duration of one cycle is about 0.8 second. Three phases succeed one another during the cycle:
a) atrial systole: 0.1 second,
b) ventricular systole: 0.3 second,
c) diastole: 0.4 second

The actual period of rest for each chamber is 0.7 second for the atria and 0.5 second for the ventricles, so in spite of its activity, the heart is at rest longer than at work.

Blood
Blood is composed of cells (corpuscles) and a liquid intercellular ground substance called plasma. The average blood volume is 5 or 6 liters (7% of body weight). Plasma constitutes about 55% of blood volume, cellular elements about 45%.

Plasma: Over 90% of plasma is water; the balance is made up of plasma proteins and dissolved electrolytes, hormones, antibodies, nutrients, and waste products. Plasma is isotonic (0.85% sodium chloride). Plasma plays a vital role in respiration, circulation, coagulation, temperature regulation, buffer activities and overall fluid balance.

Cardiovascular Conditions

The following cardiovascular information may be covered on your NSCA-CPT exam. Take the time to review the various conditions.

Cardiogenic Shock: heart is unable to meet the demands of the body. This can be caused by conduction system failure or heart muscle dysfunction.

Aortic insufficiency: Heart valve disease that prevents the aortic valve from closing completely. Backflow of blood into the left ventricle.

Aortic aneurysm: Expansion of the blood vessel wall often identified in the thoracic region.

Hypovolemic shock: Poor blood volume prevents the heart from pumping enough blood to the body.

Cardiogenic shock: Enough blood is available, however the heart is unable to move the blood in an effective manner.
Myocarditis: inflammation of the heart muscle.

Heart valve infection: endocarditis (inflammation), probable valvular heart disease. Can be caused by fungi or bacteria.

Pericarditis: Inflammation of the pericardium.

Arrhythmias: Irregular heart beats and rhythms disorder

Arteriosclerosis: hardening of the arteries.

MAJOR HORMONES

- Growth hormone- major stimulus of postnatal growth: Induces precursor cells to differentiate and secrete insulin-like growth factor I which stimulates cell division, stimulates protein synthesis;
- Insulin-stimulates fetal growth, stimulates postnatal growth by stimulating secretion of IGF-1, stimulates protein synthesis;
- Thyroid hormones-permissive for growth hormone's secretion and actions, permissive for development of the central nervous system;
- Testosterone-stimulates growth at puberty, in large part by stimulating the secretion of growth hormone, causes eventual epiphyseal closure, stimulates protein synthesis;
- Estrogen-stimulates the secretion of growth hormone at puberty, causes eventual epiphyseal closure;
- Cortisol-inhibits growth, stimulates protein catabolism.

NUTRITION

CARBOHYDRATES—SIMPLE and COMPLEX:
Carbohydrates are nutrients found in food that are the most common source of fuel for the body. After digesting carbohydrates, the body uses the resulting glucose for the brain. Additionally, carbohydrates are required for the body to break down stored fat. Carbohydrates are prominent in foods such as grains, sugars, fruits, and vegetables, as well as many refined or manufactured foods like sodas, candy, breads and pastries. Highly refined carbohydrates usually are devoid of fiber, vitamins, minerals and other micronutrients and should be eaten in very small amounts. Carbohydrates are especially important for athletes who participate in endurance sports. Carbohydrates have 4 calories per gram. Simple carbohydrates are those that are in an easy to process form, like sugar. Examples include sugars in candy, fruits, vegetables, and dairy products. Complex carbohydrates are usually combined with fiber and include foods such as breads, beans, and vegetables like potatoes and broccoli.

PROTEIN—HOW IT AFFECTS THE BODY:
Protein is a nutrient found in food that builds tissues in the body and makes hormones. Twenty-two different amino acids are necessary to make protein, and the human body only makes 13 of those, so the rest are required to be taken in as food. These 9 amino acids are considered essential amino acids. Complete proteins include all of the necessary amino acids and come from animal-based foods, such as meats. Incomplete proteins do not include all of the necessary amino acids for making proteins and are usually plant-based, such as beans or nuts. Protein has 4 calories per gram. Too much protein can cause kidney damage and elimination of calcium from the body. Athletes may need more protein because it is used as an energy source during long bouts of exercise and is needed to rebuild muscles that are worked and/or damaged.

FATS—DIFFERENT TYPES; HOW THEY ARE USED BY THE BODY:

Fat is a nutrient found in food that is necessary for energy generation; keeping the organs, skin and hair healthy; moving fat-soluble vitamins through the body; and increases the risk of many diseases when ingested in high quantities. Fat has 9 calories per gram.

Triglycerides are the primary kind of fat found in food and in the body.

Saturated fats are usually from animal-based foods, but some oils are high in saturated fats. They increase the low-density lipoproteins (LDL) in the blood, thus increasing the risk of heart disease.

Unsaturated fats are:

- Monounsaturated fats lower the levels of LDL in the blood, which lowers the risk of heart disease.
- Polyunsaturated fats can reduce the risk of heart disease.

Trans fatty acids form when unsaturated fats are turned into semi-solids. They increase LDL levels and lower high density lipoproteins (HDL), greatly increasing the risk of heart disease.

WAYS TO LOWER AMOUNT OF FAT EATEN:

- ✓ Read nutrition labels on packaged food. Determine the percentage of calories that come from fat in the food. Everyone should aim to eat less than 30% of daily calories from fat.
- ✓ Eat more fish and chicken and less red meat.
- ✓ Eat less meat overall, and instead eat more vegetarian meals.
- ✓ Eat smaller amounts of food, and eat meats that are low in fat.
- ✓ When choosing fats, choose more unsaturated fats and fewer saturated and trans-fats. If buying a product that has saturated fats, make sure there is at least double the amount of unsaturated fats as saturated fats and has very little trans fats.
- ✓ Do not fry foods, but cook in lower fat ways.
- ✓ Eat fewer snack foods.

CHOLESTEROL—DEFINITION; TWO TYPES OF LIPOPROTEINS:

Cholesterol is a nutrient that is found in animal-based food, but is also made by the body. It is necessary for the body to make cells, hormones, and bile. However, too much cholesterol in the blood is a risk factor for atherosclerosis. Eating a diet high in fat is a direct cause of having excess cholesterol in the blood. Cholesterol is transported through the body by lipoproteins. The **two types** are:

- **High density lipoproteins (HDL)** – considered "good" cholesterol, these lipoproteins help to clean the walls of the blood vessels and thus prevent atherosclerosis. A high level of HDL cholesterol lowers the risk of heart disease.
- **Low density lipoproteins (LDL)** – considered "bad" cholesterol, these lipoproteins help deposits to form on the walls of the blood vessels and thus increase the risk of atherosclerosis. A high level of LDL cholesterol is a risk factor for heart disease.

LDH vs. HDL:

When too much LDL cholesterol circulates in the blood, it can slowly build up in the inner walls of the arteries that feed the heart and brain. Together with other substances it can form plaque, a thick, hard deposit that can clog those arteries. This condition is known as atherosclerosis. If a clot forms and blocks a narrowed artery, it can cause a heart attack or stroke. The levels of HDL cholesterol and LDL cholesterol in the blood are measured to evaluate the risk of having a heart attack. LDL cholesterol of less than 100 mg/dL is the optimal level. Less than 130 mg/dL is near optimal for most people. A high LDL level (more than 160 mg/dL or 130 mg/dL or above if you have two or more risk factors for cardiovascular disease) reflects an increased risk of heart disease.

About one-third to one-fourth of blood cholesterol is carried by high-density lipoprotein (HDL). HDL cholesterol is known as the "good" cholesterol because a high level of it seems to protect against heart attack. Medical experts think that HDL tends to carry cholesterol away from the arteries and back to the liver, where it's passed from the body. Some experts believe that HDL removes excess cholesterol from plaque in arteries, thus slowing the buildup.

WATER—ITS ROLE IN THE BODY; RISKS OF DEHYDRATION; GUIDELINES FOR WATER INTAKE FOR ATHLETES AND ANYONE DOING EXERCISE:

Water in blood helps move energy in the form of glucose to all areas of the body and take waste products away from the cells through the blood, and then in the urine. Water in sweat helps to cool the body. Anyone doing strenuous workouts should make sure to drink enough water to prevent dehydration, which is the lack of enough water in the body to continue the body's processes. Early signs of dehydration are headache, getting very tired and not doing as well at the activity. Ultimately, untreated dehydration can lead to cramps, fainting, or overheating (such as heat exhaustion or heat stroke).

Guidelines for water intake are:
- ✓ Drink a half-liter of water two hours before each workout.
- ✓ Drink plenty of room temperature water during the workout.
- ✓ Someone doing endurance activities that last more than an hour should drink fluids that have added carbohydrates and electrolytes.

NUTRIENT DENSITY; GLYCEMIC INDEX; GLYCEMIC LOAD:

Nutrient density is the ratio of healthy nutrients in a food compared to the number of calories in that food. A very nutrient dense food will be low in calories and have at least 5% of the U.S. RDA of any of the recommended nutrients. Foods that are not nutrient dense will have high calories and few or no nutrients and are often called "junk" foods.

Glycemic Index is a way to determine how carbohydrates affect the levels of glucose in the blood. This is based on how fast a food is digested, how much and what kind of fiber is present, how it is prepared, how ripe it is, and what other nutrients are present. The GI is based on 50 grams of the carbohydrate. *Glycemic Load* helps determine which foods will affect blood sugar the most, by multiplying the GI by the grams of carbohydrate in the food.

DESIGNING A PROGRAM OF EATING BEFORE AND AFTER STRENUOUS EXERCISE—CARBOHYDRATE LOADING AND USING THE GLYCEMIC INDEX (GI):

By eating the right amount of carbohydrates before a workout, the body will have energy to complete the activity without using the blood glucose too soon. Foods with low GI numbers release glucose into the blood slowly and over time, while foods that have high GI numbers release glucose into the blood in a short burst soon after eating. Low GI foods are better for eating before a workout, while high GI foods are good for eating after a workout.

Carbohydrate loading uses this principle to maximize the amount of energy stored in the cells for a strenuous workout. For 3 days before an athletic event, eat a diet composed of 60-70% carbohydrates. After a workout, eat 50 grams of a low-fat carbohydrate with a high GI number immediately after finishing, and then eat another 50 grams of a similar GI level food 2 hours later.

FATS AND CARBOHYDRATES USED FOR ENERGY:

When resting, the body uses about one calorie per minute, half from carbohydrates and half from fats. During lower intensity exercise, fats and carbohydrates are used equally. Fats can only be used for energy in the presence of oxygen, so as oxygen is depleted, anaerobic systems for energy must be utilized. As the body works harder, during higher intensity exercise, fewer fats and more carbohydrate is used. Keep in mind that while exercising at lower intensities burns a greater percentage of fat, people who are trying to lose weight must increase the total number of calories used, so working at a lower intensity will not necessarily accomplish this goal.

ENERGY BALANCE—FORCES TO CONSIDER:

Energy balance means that staying at the same body weight requires that the calories taken in must be equal to the calories used. The resting metabolic rate (RMR) is the speed at which the body uses energy to maintain the processes of life (breathing, etc.). Most of the calories taken in are used for life processes. RMR is impacted by a person's age, gender, height, and activity level, but also the temperature of the air. RMR can be also be lowered if a person eats far too few calories. The activity level of a person (called the energy expended with exertion) includes the daily tasks a person does, any exercise performed, and the time immediately following exercise. The thermic effect of food is the rise in the metabolism when a person is digesting food. This is approximately 10% of the food's calorie count.

SUGGESTIONS TRAINERS CAN GIVE CLIENTS WHO WANT TO LOSE WEIGHT:

- ✓ Diet combined with exercise is the most effective weight loss strategy.
- ✓ Concentrate on changes that will increase health for life rather than short-term weight loss.
- ✓ Focus on using 500 more calories than are eaten each day.
- ✓ The person may lose momentum in the program, but that can be overcome.
- ✓ Beware of setting goals for the perfect weight.
- ✓ Even small amounts of weight loss can have enormous health benefits.
- ✓ Develop strategies for changing habits by changing shopping habits, food preparation, and restaurant choices, as well as avoiding situations where unhealthy eating is triggered.
- ✓ Instruct people about appropriate amounts of food.
- ✓ Have the person keep a log of everything she eats for a period of time in order to analyze the diet.
- ✓ Make a list of activities to do to prevent eating from being a reaction to boredom.
- ✓ It is ok to cheat occasionally, as long as the overall path is a healthy one.

THE MyPyramid SYSTEM—PROBLEMS:

The MyPyramid system recommends that half of the carbohydrates eaten in a day be whole grains, so many people may assume that they should eat half of their carbohydrates as refined flour products, although these should be strictly limited. The protein recommendations equate low-fat, natural sources of protein with high-fat, manufactured proteins, even though natural, low-fat sources are the better choice. Many people disagree that the number of dairy servings that are recommended are either too low or too high. While the online MyPyramid system is sophisticated and customized for each user, the static diagram is unclear. In addition, the online standard prevents those who do not have a computer from using the system.

WAYS IN WHICH SUPPLEMENT MANUFACTURERS MAY TRY TO REPRESENT THEIR PRODUCTS AS VALID PERFORMANCE ENHANCERS:

- ▪ The claims may be based on research with unsound designs that are not based on the scientific method.
- ▪ The package may state that studies are ongoing, which means that there is no evidence that the product works.

- The advertising may imply that the product is needed for a condition that is not necessarily a problem, nor is the product actually necessary.
- There may be testimonials or endorsements by reputable organization that did not actually endorse the product.
- The packaging may feature quotes from users of the product instead of featuring true facts about the scientific research.
- The packaging may feature a patent number and represent it as if the product was supported by the government.
- Ads for the product may be designed to look like news.
- The product may claim that more of a good thing is better.

Dietary References and Nutrition Labels

DVs (Daily Values): a new dietary reference term that will appear on the food label. It is made up of two sets of references, DRVs and RDIs.

DRVs (Daily Reference Values): a set of dietary references that applies to fat, saturated fat, cholesterol, carbohydrate, protein, fiber, sodium, and potassium.

RDIs (Reference Daily Intakes): a set of dietary references based on the Recommended Dietary Allowances for essential vitamins and minerals and, in selected groups, protein. The name "RDI" replaces the term "U.S. RDA."

RDAs (Recommended Dietary Allowances): a set of estimated nutrient allowances established by the National Academy of Sciences. It is updated periodically to reflect current scientific knowledge.

NUTRITION LABELS—THINGS TO LOOK FOR:
- ✓ Note the serving size. Many serving sizes may be much less than is actually eaten, so the number of calories and nutrients consumed must be recalculated for real world use.
- ✓ Divide the number of calories from fat by the number of total calories to determine what percentage of the total calories is from fat. Any food with more than 30% of its calories from fat may be considered a high fat food. The government defines a low fat food as one that has fewer than 3 grams of fat in a serving, so serving size must be examined carefully.
- ✓ Note whether the fats are saturated, unsaturated, or trans fats.
- ✓ Whole grain products will be indicated by the word "whole."
- ✓ Choose foods that have high fiber content.
- ✓ Avoid hidden sugars and eat food low in sugar.
- ✓ Review the RDA guidelines listed on the package.

Nutrients Key Points

I. Six Key Nutrients

1. Water
2. Protein
3. Minerals
4. Vitamins
5. Carbohydrates
6. Fats

II. Water Key Points

1. Normal production of water in a human is around 2500-2700 ml per day.
2. The average adult is composed of about 55-60% water.
3. More water is required for children and during warm weather.
4. Water acts as the body's solvent.
5. Water can be found in intra and extra cellular tissues.
6. Adults should take in 2-3 L of fluid over the course of a normal day.

III. Protein Key Points

1. Proteins are made up of amino acids.
2. Amino Acids can be broken down into essential and non-essential amino acids. At least 9 amino acids must be found in your diet and cannot be manufactured by your own body.
3. There are three types of proteins: Complete, Incomplete, and Complementary.
4. Complete proteins are found in meats, cheese and poultry. These contain all 8 essential amino acids.
5. Incomplete proteins are found in plants, nuts, grains and legumes
6. Complimentary proteins- foods that have to be combined to offer a complete protein presentation.
7. Digestion process of chymotrypsin, trypsin, carboxypeptidase, and pepsin act upon proteins.
8. Proteins help in the production of antibodies and tissue healing.
9. Proteins become an energy source if carbs/fat are not available.
10. Marasmus-starvation; recommend 15% caloric intake to be protein.
12. Uric acid, Nitrogen, and Hydrogen are all byproducts of protein breakdown.
13. Amino acids are incorporated into various structural and functional proteins, including enzymes.

High Protein Foods:
- chicken breast
- salmon
- tuna
- cottage cheese
- swordfish

- lean ground turkey
- round steak
- sirloin steak
- lean ground beef
- orange roughy
- eggs
- turkey breast
- pork
- whey
- haddock
- crab
- lobster
- shrimp

IV. Mineral Key Points

1. Minerals help maintain the function of the various acids and bases in the body.
2. About 75% of the minerals are found in bones and teeth as calcium and phosphorus.
3. Minerals may function as catalyst for cell reactions.
4. Minerals help create compounds in some cases.
5. Magnesium, Calcium, Phosphorus, Sodium and Potassium are all considered minerals
6. Minerals are usually incorporated into organic molecules, although some occur in inorganic compounds or as free ions.
7. Homeostatic mechanics regulate mineral concentration in the body.
8. Minerals are responsible for about 4% of body weight.
9. Minerals are found in all types of tissue.
10. Minerals do not create energy in the body.
11. Calcium and Phosphorus are key minerals in body development and maintenance.
12. Sodium and Potassium help trigger cell reaction potentials.
13. Minerals are found primarily in unprocessed foods.

V. Major Minerals

Calcium (Ca)
Sources: Milk, Cheese, Broccoli, Turnips
Function: Bones, Clotting, Cell wall integrity, Conduction of Nerve Impulses
Disorders: Deficient Clotting, Poor Bone Structure- Osteoporosis, Limited cell integrity.
Chlorine (Cl)
Sources: Salt
Function: Helps produce acid-base relationships that are balanced, helps with osmotic pressures and the production of hydrochloric acid, helps regulate pH.
Disorders: Excessive water loss may cause low levels of chlorine in the body.

Magnesium (Mg)
Sources: Leafy Vegetables, Whole grains, Legumes, Milk
Function: Bones, Teeth, Function as enzymes, Nerve conduction, functions in the production of ATP

Disorders: Nervous system dysfunction

Phosphorus (P)
Sources: Egg Yolk, Whole grains, Meat, Milk
Function: Helps with calcification, Maintains acid-base relationship, Works as an enzyme, occurs in the phospholipids of cell membranes
Disorders: Rickets, poor bone structure

Potassium (K)
Sources: Fruits, Whole grains, Fish and Poultry
Function: Nervous system conduction, acid-base relationship, regulation of pH
Disorders: Nausea, Weakness of muscles
Sodium (Na)
Sources: Salt, Fish, Poultry, Milk
Function: Acid-base relationship, Nerve system conduction, Uptake of glucose
Disorders: Nausea, weakness, Muscle spasms/cramping

Sulfur (S)
Sources: Egg, Cheese, Nuts, Meat
Function: Aids with B vitamin function and helps develop with development of connective tissue, found in Insulin, Biotin, and mucopolysaccharides
Disorders: None applicable.

VI. Vitamin Key Points

1. Fat- Soluble vs. Water Soluble Vitamins
2. Water Soluble – Vitamin C, B1, B2, B6, B12, Folic Acid and Niacin
3. Fat Soluble – Vitamin A, D, E, K

Water Soluble Vitamins:
Vitamin C – Ascorbic Acid
Sources: Citrus, Strawberries, Potatoes, Tomatoes
Function: Helps with uptake of iron, and cell membranes, closely related chemically to monosaccharides
Disorders: Scurvy, Anemia, Pronounced bruising of tissue

Vitamin B1- Thiamine
Sources: Legumes, Wheat germ, Pork
Function: Helps with muscle and nerve function, active in the synthesis of essential sugars
Disorders: Anorexia, nerve dysfunction, Beriberi

Vitamin B2- Riboflavin
Sources: Enriched breads, Milk, Meats, Greens
Function: Lip color, metabolic process of nutrients, eyes, can function as a coenzyme
Disorders: Weight loss, eye dysfunction, and lips may become inflamed.

Vitamin B6 - Pyridoxine
Sources: Red Meats

Function: Hemoglobin production, synthesis of proteins
Disorders: CNS disorders, kidney stones, and nausea

Vitamin B12 – Cobalamin
Sources: **Animals products only**
Function: RBC production, protein breakdown
Disorders: Pernicious anemia

Folic Acid - Folacin
Sources: Most foods.
Function: RBC production and protein breakdown, coenzyme in the synthesis of DNA
Disorders: Anemia, Stomatitis

Niacin – Nicotinic Acid
Sources: Meats, Peanut Butter
Function: Growth, Nervous System and Digestive System
Disorders: Pellagra, Dermatitis

Fat Soluble Vitamins:

Vitamin A – Retinol
Sources: Whole milk, Fish, Leafy Vegetables and Yellow Vegetables
Function: Vision, Skin, Teeth, - stored in the Liver
Disorders: Poor Vision, Xerophthalmia, Bad Skin

Vitamin D – Calciferol
Sources: Milk, Fish oils
Function: Bones. Also synthesized in the skin.
Disorders: Teeth, Bad bone structure, Rickets

Vitamin E – Tocopherol
Sources: Leafy Vegetables, Wheat germ
Function: Antioxidant, Stabilizes RBC's, stored in muscles and adipose tissue.
Disorders: Anemia, RBC's are broken down

Vitamin K – Menadione
Sources: Pork liver, Leafy Vegetables
Function: Helps with prothrombin for blood clotting
Disorders: Hemorrhagic conditions

VII. Carbohydrates Key Points

1. Three types of carbohydrates: polysaccharides, disaccharides, monosaccharides.
2. Polysaccharides- Glycogen, dietary fiber, and starch found in cereal, rice, corn and pasta.
3. Disaccharides- (double sugars) – maltose, lactose, sucrose, found in molasses, table sugar
4. Monosaccharides – (simple sugars) - Fructose, glucose, galactose found in fruit and honey
5. Energy is released from glucose by oxidation.
6. If inadequate amounts of glucose are available, amino acids may be converted to glucose.

7. Carbohydrates provide energy and help in the breakdown of fat.
8. Carbohydrates can only be used the form of simple sugars by the body.
9. Primary processing and uptake of carbohydrates occurs in the small intestine by the enzymes maltase, sucrase, and lactase.
10. Glucose is the simple sugar used by the CNS and glucose can be stored as glycogen (polysaccharide) until being used later.
11. High levels of carbohydrates can lead to weight gain, and poor nutritional status.
12. Studies indicate that approximately 55% of an adults intake is carbohydrates.
13. Carbohydrates are absorbed as monosaccharides.
14. Dietary fiber can be broken down into soluble and insoluble dietary fiber.
15. Glucose is regulated by Insulin and Glucagon (horomone).
16. Educate clients to reduce simple sugars and encourage clients to eat more complex carbohydrates.

VIII. Fat Key Points

1. Excessive fats can lead to weight gain, stroke, and heart disease.
2. There are two primary types of fat: saturated fats and unsaturated fats.
3. Saturated fats- completely maximized number of Hydrogen present. Examples: eggs, chocolate, dairy, coconut oil, meats, usually solid at room temperature.
4. Unsaturated fats- usually liquid at room temperature, do not have maximum number of Hydrogen atoms present. Examples: soybean and corn oil.
5. Fats provide insulation to the body.
6. Linoleic acid is an essential fatty acid.
7. Cholesterol is obtained in foods of animal origin only.
8. Fats help with the transportation of fat soluable vitamins.
9. Fats act as an energy source when carbohydrates are unavailable.
10. Fats help create linoleic acid which is an essential component not created in the human body.
11. Primary fat breakdown occurs in the small intestine, however, some is performed in the stomach by gastric lipase.
12. Fats can also be classified as visible or invisible.
13. Visible fats: Shortening, Meats, Margarine, Butter
14. Invisible fats: Cheese, Milk, Avocado
15. Recommend to your clients total intake of fat to be less than 30% of caloric intake.
16. Cholesterol is a fatty type complex and is found in healthy adults.
17. Cholesterol is divided into (HDL) and (LDL) cholesterol.
18. HDL- High density lipoprotein
19. LDL- Low density lipoprotein
20. High Cholesterol is noted as above 240mg/dl
21. Borderline – 200-240 mg/dl
22. <200 mg/dl Recommended
23. Recommend polyunsaturated fats to lower cholesterol levels to your clients.

1 g Carbohydrates = 4 Calories
1 g Protein = 4 Calories
1 g Fat = 9 Calories

EATING DISORDERS

CHARACTERISTICS TO LOOK FOR:
Symptoms of anorexia nervosa:
- Strong fear of gaining weight, even while losing weight.
- Having a distorted view of her body fat compared to reality
- Losing more than 15% of starting weight.
- Continuing to strive for weight loss even after dropping below healthy standards.
- Absence of disease that would cause these symptoms.

Symptoms of bulimia nervosa:
- Overeating junk foods in short bursts, sometimes hiding the behavior
- The person makes himself vomit, or may fall asleep or have stomach pain after overeating incident.
- Attempting to lose weight by vomiting, using laxatives or diuretics
- Weight going up and down by more than 10 pounds.
- Depression and low-self image

Symptoms of binge-eating disorder:
- Overeating incidents on 2 or more days per week for 6 months with no purging afterwards.
- Eating fast, eating by herself, or eating even though not hungry.
- Low self-image

ANOREXIA vs. BULIMIA:
One of two common eating disorders, anorexia is a condition in which a person refuses to eat sufficient food to maintain a minimum normal weight for age and height. The consequent wasting away has serious effects on many body systems, and may result in death. A weight loss of 25% is one criterion for diagnosing anorexia.

Bulimia is an eating disorder marked by cycles of binge eating of excessive quantities of food, followed by purging using vomiting, laxatives or diuretics. Unlike anorexia, a person with bulimia is rarely grossly underweight. The purging can seriously damage health. The gastric acid from vomiting excoriates sensitive oesophageal mucosa; excessive laxative and diuretic use can impair body electrolyte balance, bowel and kidney function. Bulimia tends to start in late teens and older age groups.

Physical Effects of Anorexia:
    Loss of menstrual periods
    Significant bone density loss (osteoporosis)
    Dry, brittle nails and hair
    Lowered resistance to illness
    Hypersensitivity to heat and cold
    Appears to need less sleep than normal eaters
    Muscle loss and weakness
    Severe dehydration, which can result in kidney failure
    Fainting, fatigue, and overall weakness

Emotional Effects:
    Difficulty in concentrating on anything.

Isolation from family and friends
Irritability
Feelings of guilt and depression
Dependence upon alcohol or drugs to handle the negative outlook

WELLNESS

WELLNESS—ITS RELATIONSHIP TO HEALTH:
Wellness is a lifestyle model that includes a person's bodily, religious, and psychological health. It can be perceived as a means to prevention of disease by performing actions that reduce a person's likelihood of developing certain conditions. In addition, wellness is a goal for the best possible health and functioning of the whole person. Wellness is often mistaken for only a healthy diet and exercise routine, but it is more than that. It is an ongoing lifestyle, not an achievable or static state of being. Wellness can be expressed as a continuum ranging from death to optimal health and satisfaction in life.

CANCER—FORMS WHICH MAY BE PREVENTABLE THRU LIFESTYLES CHOICES:
Cancer is any of a number of diseases in which mutated cells grow in an irregular way and may proliferate throughout the body. Many cancers may be averted by changes in lifestyle. Cancer of the lung, breast, colon and rectum, pancreas, skin, bladder, esophagus, pharynx, mouth, tongue, cervix and liver have been determined to have possible causes in behaviors. Smoking cessation is the single greatest lifestyle change that would reduce cancer risk, particularly in the lung, pancreas, tongue, esophagus, pharynx, mouth, and bladder, as well as leukemia. Wearing sunscreen or staying out of the sun would eliminate most skin cancer risk. Reducing the use of alcohol and eating a diet low in fat and high in fiber would reduce the risk of liver, breast, and colon cancer. Cervical cancer can be prevented by avoiding the human papilloma virus either through vaccination or abstinence.

DIABETES—TYPE 1 and TYPE 2:
Insulin is used to move glucose (sugar in the blood that can be used as energy) into the body's cells. Diabetes is a condition in which the body doesn't use insulin properly. If the cells do not react properly to insulin, too much glucose will remain in the blood instead of moving into the cells, a condition called hyperglycemia or high blood sugar. People with Type 1 diabetes do not make enough insulin, and must inject themselves with insulin in order to move glucose into the cells. People with Type 2 diabetes, also called non-insulin dependent diabetes mellitus (NIDDM), make enough insulin, but their cells do not respond effectively to insulin and so glucose is not moved efficiently into the cells. Type 2 diabetes can often be controlled or prevented by eating more dietary fiber and by becoming more active. Exercise has been shown to increase the effectiveness of insulin.

BENEFITS OF CARDIORESPIRATORY FITNESS:
Lower risk of cardiovascular disease:
- ✓ Lower pressure on arterial walls
- ✓ Higher levels of high-density lipoproteins
- ✓ Lower levels of triglycerides in blood
- ✓ Less body fat
- ✓ More efficient use of insulin and better blood sugar uptake
- ✓ Better blood clotting

Better functioning of heart, blood vessels, and lungs:
- ✓ More oxygen brought into the body and made available to cells
- ✓ More blood pumped with each beat
- ✓ Stronger heart muscle

✓ Heart beats slower and arterial pressure reduced
✓ More capillaries to bring blood to muscles
✓ Better ability to make more energy with oxygen before switching to non-oxygen energy pathways
✓ Ability to do activities for longer and with more vigor

Additional advantages:
✓ Less likelihood for mental illness
✓ Feeling calmer and happier
✓ Better ability to perform sports or other activities
✓ Better functioning for senior citizens
✓ More restful sleep
✓ Increased ability to fight disease
✓ Better attitude and feelings about life
✓ Lower risk of disease or death

TACTICS FOR MOTIVATING A PERSON TO BEGIN AN EXERCISE PROGRAM:

- Focus on the good health results that will come with the program.
- Get assistance from a doctor as a knowledgeable expert.
- Do not push the person to work too hard too early in the program.
- Develop a system of rewards to help motivate the person.
- Update the person on his progress frequently, focusing on successes.
- Warn the person that he is likely to falter in his progress, but that any problems can be overcome. Plan for those barriers that are predictable.
- Develop a system of reminders to exercise, whether making appointments or finding ways to trigger the activity.
- Have the person sign a contract with himself to do the activity.
- Show the person how the exercise can be worked into daily life, even without a trainer to motivate him.
- Find interesting activities to stimulate the person.
- Work to reduce the risk of injury.
- Model good health habits.

STAGES IN THE TRANSTHEORETICAL MODEL OF CHANGE:

- **Stage One** – Precontemplation stage – This is a period in which the person is not even considering any exercise program or lifestyle change.
- **Stage Two** – Contemplation stage – This period is one in which a person is thinking about starting an exercise program, or making another lifestyle change.
- **Stage Three** – Preparation stage – During this period, the person may actually take small actions to begin the change, such as calling personal trainers for information or planning to start an exercise program within a few weeks.
- **Stage Four** – Action stage – During this period, the person begins the new activity. For the first 6 months of any new activity, dropout rates are very high, so this is a vulnerable stage.
- **Stage Five** – Maintenance stage – This period is one in which the person has made the activity a habit and continues doing it over time.

SOCIAL COGNITIVE THEORY:

Social Cognitive Theory proposes that a behavior is impacted by the situation and surroundings and the person's experiences and beliefs. One key component is a person's self-efficacy, which means the person's belief that he or she can do something.

Four ways to improve self-efficacy are:

1. Having successful experiences with the behavior.
2. Watching other people do well with the behavior.
3. Hearing supportive affirmation of success.
4. Seeing real and quantifiable accomplishments as a result of the behavior.

Another key component is the concept of having realistic outcome expectations. A person will not succeed if his expectations of the result are impossible or highly unlikely. Setting suitable goals is an important requirement of success.

APPROACH GOALS and AVOIDANCE GOALS; S.M.A.R.T. SYSTEM OF GOAL SETTING; INTRINSIC AND EXTRINSIC MOTIVATION:

Approach goals are aspirations to do something, while **avoidance goals** are aspirations to keep away from something. Approach goals are generally more effective. The **SMART system** stands for goals that are Specific, Measurable, Action-oriented, Realistic and relevant, and Timed. All of these features should be considered when setting reachable goals. It is best to set goals that are easily reachable, so that those successes can help define future goals. When planning an activity program with a person, goals should be redefined as they are reached. **Intrinsic motivation** comes from within the person, based on their beliefs, experiences, self-efficacy, etc. **Extrinsic motivation** comes from outside the person, such as another person or a situation.

PERFORMANCE

PERFORMANCE ABILITIES/LIMITATIONS—UNCONTROLLABLE FACTORS:

Because longer arms or legs are farther away from the joints, they must move a longer distance in each joint motion, and therefore cannot move as much weight. A person with shorter arms and legs has the potential to lift more weight than another person with similar musculature but longer arms and legs. People with tendons that attach farther away from the joint will be able to lift more weight. People with longer muscles will be able to lift more weight. People with more fast twitch muscle fibers will be able to lift more weight. Men in general, or women with more testosterone, will be able to lift more weight because of testosterone making muscles bigger. The increase in muscle strength due to exercise will vary in each person based on the body's genetic ability to adapt.

COMMON PROBLEMS IN FOLLOWING AN ACTIVITY PROGRAM—DIFFERENT LEVELS:

Beginners –
- may have a difficult time balancing or doing activities which require a powerful torso to keep the body still;
- may find it difficult to determine which muscles to contract to move in new ways;
- may work too hard, thus becoming sore and possibly quitting the program;
- may not recognize the difference between expected muscle soreness and the pain of injury.
- need uncomplicated directions.

Intermediate clients –
- should be given more specifics about the exercises you are recommending;

- as they become more fit they will begin doing more complicated exercises to work smaller muscle groups;
- may reach a point in which improvements are not as noticeable and may remain at that level for some time.

Advanced clients –
- may try more difficult and risky maneuvers in order to improve their fitness or train for a specific sport, so they should be reminded of safety concerns.

ASSISTANCE—MAINTAINED TOUCH, PALPATION, KNIFE-EDGE TOUCH, MOVE-AWAY TOUCH, AND MOVE-TOWARDS TOUCH:

Maintained touch is holding a hand on a body part as a reminder to the person to hold a particular position. *Palpation* is the act of wiggling the fingers on a body part or muscle to demonstrate to the person which muscle is being worked. The *knife-edge touch* involves dragging the side of the hand along a part of the body to demonstrate the way a muscle contraction is going. The *move-away touch* involves having the person retreat from your hand when doing the activity. The *move-towards touch* involves having the person go in the direction of your hand when doing an activity.

PROMPTS/CUES:

Prompts, or cues, can be given through speaking, touching, or from eye contact during a workout so as to keep the person motivated, reduce awkwardness from not speaking at all, and to enhance the training experience. An *alignment cue* reminds the person about how to position a joint or muscle during the activity. An *educational or informational cue* gives the person additional facts about the activity or how it will improve their life outside of the workout. A *safety cue* reminds the person how to prevent injury during a particular activity.
A *breathing cue* emphasizes proper breathing techniques. A *motivational or affirmational cue* encourages the person to continue and recognizes their current effort and accomplishment.

PROMPTS—ADDITIONAL CUES:

An *imagery cue* guides a person to picture in their head a different way of perceiving the exercise that may be easier to understand. A *visual cue* means showing the person how to do an exercise, either by doing the exercise yourself or by showing a picture. A *wrong/right cue* is showing the person the improper way to do the activity so she can feel the wrong way to do it, then showing her the proper way to do the activity. A *tactile cue* is any cue that involves touch. The trainer may put his/her hands on the person to demonstrate something, or the person may touch the trainer while he/she performs an action.

PERFORMANCE ENHANCERS—ERGOGENIC AID, PLACEBO EFFECT, ANABOLIC STEROIDS, HUMAN GROWTH HORMONE:

An *ergogenic aid* is anything that is believed to enhance a person's ability to do a sport or other physical activity. The *placebo effect* is the improvement that is often seen in athletic performance (or general health) when the person taking a substance believes the sub-stance is helping his or her performance. This may reflect more improvement than the substance actually gives the body. *Anabolic steroids* are chemicals made in a laboratory that resemble testosterone. They can make muscles bigger, and stronger, but can lead to increased anger, larger breasts in men, smaller breasts in women, heart problems, cancer and infertility. *Human growth hormone* (hGH) is a natural chemical made by the body that lowers fat and makes muscle. Used in large quantities, it can result in the feet, hands and face getting larger and the skin getting thicker, retaining fluids, inefficient use of insulin, and high blood pressure.

PERFORMANCE ENHANCERS—CREATINE, BLOOD DOPING, AND CAFFEINE:
Creatine is a chemical that seems to improve brief, vigorous activity, but has no effect on activities that last for longer periods of time. It may be damaging to the kidneys. ***Blood doping*** is the practice of increasing the amount of red blood cells in the body (usually by adding concentrated blood to the body). This can help a person use more oxygen (which is moved through the body in the red blood cells), but can also lead to heart attack, or spread of blood-borne illnesses. ***Caffeine*** is a chemical found naturally that increases a person's feeling of energy, increases heart rate, and can help someone perform an activity for longer periods of time. Caffeine is a reasonably safe chemical, but in high doses can cause sleeplessness or feelings of anxiousness.

Ergogenic Aids

Caffeine
The most important effect of caffeine may be in mobilising fatty acids, which can then be used as a fuel, sparing the glycogen stores. This may benefit the endurance athlete, but the diuretic effect of caffeine may be harmful, especially in the heat.

Caffeine is also a stimulant, and may help power events, while the diuretic property will lead to a loss of weight which could be beneficial in certain events, for example high jumping, long jumping and pole-vaulting.

Creatine
Reports have suggested that creatine levels in skeletal muscle can be increased, and performance of high intensity exercise enhanced, following a period of creatine supplementation. However, neither endurance exercise performance nor maximal oxygen uptake appear to be enhanced.

Although creatine is normally present in the diet (in meat and fish), the amounts (about 1 gram per day) are much less than the 20 g/day which has been shown to enhance performance when taken for 5-6 days.

Creatine is an amino acid that occurs naturally in the body and:
- Aids in ATP resynthesis;
- Maintains ATP/ADP ratios;
- In combination with phosphorous (PCr) buffers the accumulation of H+ (what athletes commonly refer to as lactic acid) during periods of intense exercise;
- Facilitates high energy phosphate transport from the mitochondria to the contractile proteins of skeletal muscle.

Sodium Bicarbonate
Sodium bicarbonate is an alkaline salt found naturally in the body. Sodium bicarbonate in the blood is referred to as the alkaline reserve. The alkaline reserve is responsible for buffering lactic acid which builds up in the muscles during intense exercise and is a key factor in fatigue.

Numerous studies have shown that sodium bicarbonate supplements can delay the onset of fatigue.

Ergogenic aids fall into the following categories:

Mechanical Aids
  Altitude Training
  Heart Rate Monitors
  Computers - analyse VO2 max, technique, test results etc
  Video recorders - analyse technique
  Tyre towing - develop strength
  Weights - develop strength
  Hypoxic Tents
  Nasal Strips
  Parachutes - develop strength
  Elastic cord (pulling)- develop speed
  Elastic cord (restraining) - develop strength
  Downhill running (3° to 5° slope) - develop speed
  Uphill running (5° to 10° slope) - develop strength
  Treadmills
  Weighted vests (5% to 8% of body weight) - develop strength
  Sports clothing, footwear and equipment
  Timing equipment

Pharmacological Aids
  Supplements

Physiological Aids
  Creatine
  Colostrum
  Sports Massage
  Physiotherapy
  Herbal Medicines
  Acupuncture
  Sauna
  Ultra-violet rays

Nutritional Aids
  Carbohydrate Loading
  Caffeine
  Creatine
  Bicarbonate of Soda
  Sports Drinks

Psychological Aids
  Cheering
  Hypnosis
  Psychology
  Music
  Relaxation
  Imagery

Illegal Ergogenic Aids:

> *Physiological*
>> Blood Doping
>> EPO
>
> *Pharmaceutical*
>> Amphetamine
>> Beta Blocker
>> Human Growth Hormone
>> Anabolic Steroid
>> Masking agents
>> Diuretic

The major side effects of anabolic steroid use include liver tumors, jaundice, fluid retention, and high blood pressure; others are severe acne and trembling. Additional side effects include the following:

For men - shrinking of the testicles, reduced sperm count, infertility, baldness, development of breasts.

For women - growth of facial hair, changes in or cessation of the menstrual cycle, enlargement of the clitoris, deepened voice.

General Side Effects of Anabolic Steroids are:

- Liver damage
- Kidney failure
- Testicular atrophy and infertility
- Prostatic hypertrophy, which can cause problems later in life
- Enlargement of the female clitoris
- Increase in cholesterol
- Premature closure of epiphyses in long bones, especially in younger users
- Acne
- Hastening of male-pattern baldness
- Deepening of female voice, increase in facial hair
- Gynecomastia, which could lead to: impotence, apathy, decrease in sex drive, chronic water retention

AXIAL SKELETON

The axial skeleton consists of 80 bones forming the trunk (spine and thorax) and skull.

Vertebral Column: The main trunk of the body is supported by the spine, or vertebral column, which is composed of 26 bones, some of which are formed by the fusion of a few bones. The vertebral column from superior to inferior consists of 7 cervical (neck), 12 thoracic and 5 lumbar vertebrae, as well as a sacrum, formed by fusion of 5 sacral vertebrae, and a coccyx, formed by fusion of 4 coccygeal vertebrae.

Ribs and Sternum: The axial skeleton also contains 12 pairs of *ribs* attached posteriorly to the thoracic vertebrae and anteriorly either directly or via cartilage to the *sternum* (breastbone). The ribs and sternum form the *thoracic cage*, which protects the heart and lungs. Seven pairs of ribs articulate with the sternum (*fixed ribs*) directly, and three do so via cartilage; the two most inferior pairs do not attach anteriorly and are referred to as *floating ribs*.

Skull: The skull consists of 22 bones fused together to form a rigid structure which houses and protects organs such as the brain, auditory apparatus and eyes. The bones of the skull form the *face* and *cranium* (brain case) and consist of 6 single bones (*occipital, frontal, ethmoid, sphenoid, vomer* and *mandible*) and 8 paired bones (*parietal, temporal, maxillary, palatine, zygomatic, lacrimal, inferior concha* and *nasal*). The *lower jaw* or *mandible* is the only movable bone of the skull (head); it articulates with the temporal bones.

Other Parts: Other bones considered part of the axial skeleton are the *middle ear bones* (*ossicles*) and the small U-shaped *hyoid bone* that is suspended in a portion of the neck by muscles and ligaments.

APPENDICULAR SKELETON

The *appendicular skeleton* forms the major internal support of the appendages—the *upper* and *lower extremities* (limbs).

Pectoral Girdle and Upper Extremities: The arms are attached to and suspended from the axial skeleton via the *shoulder* (*pectoral*) *girdle*. The latter is composed of two *clavicles* (*collarbones*) and two *scapulae* (*shoulder blades*). The clavicles articulate with the sternum; the two *sternoclavicular joints* are the only sites of articulation between the trunk and upper extremity.

Each upper limb from distal to proximal (closest to the body) consists of hand, wrist, forearm and arm (upper arm). The *hand* consists of 5 *digits* (fingers) and 5 *metacarpal* bones. Each digit is composed of three bones called *phalanges*, except the thumb which has only two bones.

Pelvic Girdle and Lower Extremities: The lower *extremities*, or legs, are attached to the axial skeleton via the *pelvic* or *hip girdle*. Each of the two coxal, or *hip bones* comprising the pelvic girdle is formed by the fusion of three bones—*illium, pubis,* and *ischium*. The coxal bones attach the lower limbs to the trunk by articulating with the sacrum.

Part of the Skeleton	Number of Bones
Axial Skeleton	80
Skull	22
Ossicles (malleus, incus and stapes)	6
Vertebral column	26
Ribs	24
Sternum	1
Hyoid	1
Appendicular Skeleton	126
Upper extremities	64
Lower extremities	62

CHARACTERISTICS OF BONE

Bone is a specialized type of connective tissue consisting of cells (*osteocytes*) embedded in a calcified matrix which gives bone its characteristic hard and rigid nature. Bones are encased by a *periosteum*, a connective tissue sheath. All bone has a central marrow cavity. *Bone marrow* fills the marrow cavity or smaller marrow spaces, depending on the type of bone.

Types of Bone: There are two types of bone in the skeleton: *compact bone* and *spongy* (cancellous) bone.

Compact Bone. *Compact bone* lies within the periosteum, forms the outer region of bones, and appears dense due to its compact organization. The living osteocytes and calcified matrix are arranged in layers, or *lamellae*. Lamellae may be circularly arranged surrounding a central canal, the *Haversian canal*, which contains small blood vessels.

Spongy Bone. *Spongy bone* consists of *bars, spicules* or *trabeculae*, which forms a lattice meshwork. Spongy bone is found at the ends of long bones and the inner layer of flat, irregular and short bones. The trabeculae consist of osteocytes embedded in calcified matrix, which in definitive bone has a lamellar nature. The spaces between the trabeculae contain bone marrow.

Bone Cells: The cells of bone are osteocytes, osteoblasts, and osteoclasts. *Osteocytes* are found singly in *lacunae* (spaces) within the calcified matrix and communicate with each other via small canals in the bone known as *canaliculi*. The latter contain osteocyte cell processes. The osteocytes in compact and spongy bone are similar in structure and function.

Osteoblasts are cells which form bone matrix, surrounding themselves with it, and thus are transformed into osteocytes. They arise from undifferentiated cells, such as mesenchymal cells. They are cuboidal cells which line the trabeculae of immature or developing spongy bone.

Osteoclasts are cells found during bone development and remodeling. They are multinucleated cells lying in cavities, *Howship's lacunae*, on the surface of the bone tissue being resorbed. Osteoclasts remove the existing calcified matrix releasing the inorganic or organic components.

Bone Matrix: *Matrix* of compact and spongy bone consists of collagenous fibers and ground substance which constitute the organic component of bone. Matrix also consists of inorganic material which is about 65% of the dry weight of bone. Approximately 85% of the inorganic component consists of calcium phosphate in a crystalline form (hydroxyapatite crystals). Glycoproteins are the main components of the ground substance.

MAJOR TYPES OF HUMAN BONES

Type of Bone	Characteristics	Examples
Long bones	Width less than length	Humerus, radius, ulna, femur, tibia
Short bones	Length and width close to equal in size	Carpal and tarsal bones
Flat bones	Thin flat shape	Scapulae, ribs, sternum, bones of cranium (occipital, frontal, parietal)
Irregular bones	Multifaceted shape	Vertebrae, sphenoid, ethmoid ---------
Sesamoid	Small bones located in tendons of muscles	

JOINTS

The bones of the skeoeton articulate with each other at *joints*, which are variable in structure and function. Some joints are immovable, such as the *sutures* between the bones of the cranium. Others are *slightly movable joints*; examples are the *intervertebral joints* and the *pubic symphysis* (joint between the two pubic bones of the coxal bones).

TYPES OF JOINTS

Joint Type	Characteristic	Example
Ball and socket	Permits all types of movement (abduction, adduction, flexion, extension, circumduction); it is considered a universal joint.	Hips and shoulder joints
Hinge (ginglymus)	Permits motion in one plane only	Elbow and knee, interphalangeal joints
Rotating or pivot	Rotation is only motion permitted	Radius and ulna, atlas and axis (first and second cervical vertebrae)
Plane or gliding	Permits sliding motion	Between tarsal bones and carpal bones
Condylar (condyloid)	Permits motion in two planes which are at right angles to each other (rotation is not possible)	Metacarop-phalangeal joints, temporomandibular

Adjacent bones at a joint are connected by fibrous connective tissue bands known as *ligaments*. They are strong bands which support the joint and may also act to limit the degree of motion occurring at a joint.

BONES/JOINTS and MUSCLES—DESCRIPTIONS; JOINT ACTION; MAJOR MUSCLES; MOVEMENTS PERFORMED

SHOULDER GIRDLE; MAIN JOINT ACTIONS:
The shoulder girdle is made of the bones of the clavicle and shoulder blades (scapulae). The joint between these bones is called the scapulothoracic joint.
The main joint actions of the shoulder girdle are:
- Scapular elevation – the shoulder girdle moves up
- Scapular depression – the shoulder girdle moves down
- Scapular retraction (also called scapular adduction) – the shoulder girdle moves
- backward and the scapulae are pulled together.
- Scapular protraction (also called scapular abduction) – the shoulder girdle moves
- forward and the scapulae are pulled apart
- Scapular upward rotation – the scapula turns upward as the clavicles are elevated (arms lifted in front of the body).
- Scapular downward rotation – the reverse of the scapular upward rotation.
- Scapular upward tilt – the top of the scapula turns forward while the bottom moves
- backward and out from the ribs.
- Scapular reduction of upward tilt – the reverse of the scapular upward tilt.

SHOULDER GIRDLE—MAJOR MUSCLES; MAIN MOVEMENTS:

- The trapezius muscle is divided into four parts. Parts I and II (together called the upper trapezius) are involved in scapular elevation (shoulder shrugs). Part II (called the middle trapezius) is involved in scapular retraction (shoulder blades pulling together). Part IV (called the lower trapezius) is involved in scapular depression (shoulders moving down) and in upward rotation (arms lifted in front of the body).
- The rhomboids are under the trapezius and are involved in scapular retraction, scapular downward rotation (arms lowered in front of body), and shoulder shrugs.
- The serratus anterior attaches to the ribs and is involved in scapular protraction (shoulder blades pulling apart from each other) and lifting the arms in front of the body.
- The pectoralis minor is under the pectoralis major and is involved in moving the shoulders down, pulling the shoulder blades apart, and lowering the arms in front of the body.
- Levator scapulae is involved in shoulder shrugs.
- Subclavius is involved in moving the shoulders down.

LATISSMUS DORSI and ROTATOR CUFF MUSCLES:

The **latissmus dorsi** (lats) spread across the back and attach below the arm. They are involved in shoulder extension (pushing arms straight out behind the body) and shoulder adduction (lowering the arms while out to the side). The **rotator cuff muscles** are 4 muscles that form a ring (like the cuff of a sleeve) around the shoulder. The four rotator cuff muscles are the supraspinatus, the infraspinatus, teres minor and subscapularis. Supraspinatus is involved in shoulder abduction (raising arms while out to the side). Subscapularis is involved in shoulder internal rotation. Infraspinatus and teres minor are involved in shoulder external rotation.

PECTORALIS MAJOR and DELTOIDS:

Pectoralis major is a big muscle attaching to the front of the chest and crossing across the shoulder to the upper arm. It is involved in shoulder horizontal flexion (or adduction), in which the arm is held straight out to the side of the body (horizontally) and moves to the front of the body. It also works the reverse action, in which the arm returns to the side, called shoulder horizontal extension (or abduction). **The deltoids** are a 3-part muscle at the uppermost part of the shoulder, made up of the anterior, medial and posterior deltoids. These are involved in shoulder flexion (hold arms in front of body and raise them overhead), shoulder extension (push arms straight behind the body and lift), shoulder abduction (raising arms while out to the side), shoulder adduction (lowering arms out to the side) and shoulder horizontal flexion and shoulder horizontal extension.

ELBOW JOINTS; MAIN JOINT ACTIONS:

- The humeroulnar joint joins the ulna and the humerus and is involved in elbow flexion (bending arm up and toward the body as if curling a hand weight) and elbow extension (straightening arm back out).
- The radioulnar joints join the top and bottom of the radius and ulna bones in the forearm. The humeroradial joint joins the humerus and radius bones. These joints work together in radioulnar supination, which is a motion of rotating the forearm until the palm is facing up. In this motion, the ulna and radius bones of the forearm will be parallel. The joints also work together for the reverse motion, in rotating the forearm to face the palm down. In this motion, the ulna and radius bones of the forearm will cross each other slantways.

ELBOW JOINTS—MAJOR MUSCLES; MAIN MOVEMENTS:

- The biceps brachii is the biggest muscle in the arm, attaching at the elbow and shoulder. It is involved in elbow flexion (the biceps curl exercise) and helps in shoulder flexion (holding arms in front of the body and lifting them overhead).
- The brachialis, under the biceps brachii, and the brachioradialis in the forearm are involved in elbow flexion.
- The triceps brachii is opposite the biceps brachii. It attaches to the shoulder at three points and is involved in elbow extension (straightening arm from elbow flexion), and helps push the arms back behind the shoulders and lower the arms out to the side (shoulder adduction).
- The anconeus lies behind the elbow and is involved in elbow extension.
- The supinator in the forearm is involved in radialulnar supination (rotating forearm to palm up position).
- The pronator quadratus and pronator teres in the forearm are involved in radioulnar pronation (rotating forearm to palm down position).

SPINE— FORMATION; MAIN JOINT ACTIONS:

The spine is formed from 33 bones called vertebrae arranged on top of one another and forming 4 curves. Seven vertebrae make up the cervical curve, 12 vertebrae make up the thoracic curve, and 5 vertebrae make up the lumbar curve. The sacral curve is made of 5 vertebrae that are combined to make the sacrum and 4 combined vertebrae make up the tailbone (also called the coccyx).

The main joint actions of the spine are:
- Spinal flexion, where the spine curves forward with the neck moving toward the chest
- Spinal extension, where the spine curves backward with the neck tilted back and the head up.
- Spinal rotation, in which the spine twists to the side
- Spinal lateral flexion, in which the spine and torso are bent to the side

SPINE—MAJOR MUSCLES; MAIN MOVEMENTS:

- The rectus abdominus spreads up the abdomen from the pelvis to the ribs. It is involved in spinal flexion (the "sit up" movement).
- The external and internal obliques spread slantways across the abdomen. They are involved in spinal flexion with rotation (a cross-over sit-up), and as helpers in spinal lateral flexion (bending to the side).
- The transverse abdominus is located deep in the abdomen and is used in abdominal compression ("holding in" the muscles of the abdomen).
- The erector spinae comprises three muscle pairs, the iliocostalis, longissimus, and spinalis that straddle the spine. They are involved in spinal extension (curving the spine backward).
- The multifidi lie under the erector spinae and help to steady the spine. They are involved in spinal extension and spinal rotation (twisting the torso).
- The quadratus lumborum attaches to the lower ribs to the pelvis and is involved in bending to the side.

PELVIC GIRDLE—MAIN JOINT ACTIONS; MUSCLES; MAIN MOVEMENTS:

The pelvic girdle is the set of bones that connects the torso to the legs. When the pelvic girdle moves, it triggers motion in the spine and the hip joint.

Its main joint actions are:
- ✓ the anterior pelvic tilt (the tailbone is thrust outward),
- ✓ the posterior pelvic tilt (the tailbone is "tucked" under the spine),

✓ the lateral pelvic tit (hip thrust out to one side).

The muscles of the pelvic girdle are also muscles of the spine or hip joint.

- Hip flexors and erector spinae are involved in thrusting the tailbone outward.
- The gluteus maximus, hamstrings, and rectus abdominus are involved in tucking the tailbone under the spine.
- The quadratus lumborum, gluteus medius and hip adductors are involved in thrusting the hip to one side.

HIP JOINT; MAIN JOINT ACTIONS:

The hip joint joins the pelvis and the femur (hip bone) in a ball and socket arrangement that resembles the shoulder joint.

Its main joint actions are:
- ✓ Hip flexion – lifting the thigh in front of the body
- ✓ Hip extension – lowering the thigh or pushing to the back of the body
- ✓ Hip abduction – swinging the hip and thigh straight out to the side
- ✓ Hip adduction – pulling the hip and thigh straight in toward the opposite leg
- ✓ Hip internal rotation – knee turned in toward opposite knee
- ✓ Hip external rotation – knee turned out to the side
- ✓ Hip circumduction – leg circles

HIP JOINT—MAIN MUSCLES:

- The iliopsoas muscle (hip flexors) is two muscles acting together (the iliacus and psoas muscles) that connect to the leg, spread over the pelvis and attach to the spine.
- The gluteus maximus is the biggest muscle in the buttocks.
- The hamstrings are three muscles, the biceps femoris, semitendinosus, and semimembranosus, which interact with the hip and knee joints and are located in the back of the leg.
- The gluteus medius is located at the top of the hip.
- The hip adductors are five muscles (adductor longus, adductor brevis, adductor magnus, gracilis, and pectineus).
- The gluteus minimus lies below the gluteus medius.
- The hip outward rotators are six muscles (piriformis, obturator internus, obturator externus, quadratus femoris, gemellus superior, and gemellus inferior) located deep in the buttocks.

HIP JOINT—MAIN MOVEMENTS OF MUSCLES:

- The iliopsoas muscle is involved in lifting the thigh in front of the body (hip flexion).
- The gluteus maximus is involved in pushing the thigh down and back (hip extension) and turning the knee to the side (hip external rotation).
- The hamstrings are involved in pushing the thigh down and back.
- The gluteus medius is involved in swinging the hip and thigh out to the side (hip abduction).
- The hip adductors are involved in pulling the thigh and hip in toward the opposite leg (hip adduction). The pectineus muscle (one of the hip adductors) is involved in lifting the thigh in front of the body (hip flexion).
- The gluteus minimus is involved in turning the knee inward (hip internal rotation) and swinging the hip and thigh out to the side (hip abduction).
- The hip outward rotators are involved in turning the knee out to the side (hip external rotation).

KNEE JOINT—MAIN JOINT ACTIONS; MAIN MUSCLES and MOVEMENTS:
The knee joint is the point where the thigh bone (femur) and leg bone (tibia) meet in a complex hinge joint. The knee joint is distinctive because the menisci (semilunar cartilages) that cushion the area between the bones allow a great deal of pressure to push on the knee. The main joint actions of the knee joint are straightening the knee and bending the knee.

The main muscles of the knee joint are:
- The quadriceps are four muscles (vastus lateralis, vastus medialis, vastus intermedius, and rectus femoris) that attach near the kneecap (patella) and are involved in straightening the knee. The rectus femoris is involved in lifting the thigh in front of the body.
- The hamstrings attach to the hip joint and the knee and are involved in bending the knee.
- The popliteus is a small muscle in the back of the knee that is involved in bending the knee.

ANKLE JOINT; MAIN JOINT ACTIONS:
The ankle joint is a combination of two joints, the talocrural joint and the subtalar joint. The talocrural joint is the point where the tibia and fibula meet the talus. The subtalar joint is the point where the talus meets the heel. The main joint actions of the talocrural joint are ankle dorsiflexion (flexing the foot and toes back toward the leg) and ankle plantar flexion (curling the foot downward). The main joint actions of the subtalar joint are ankle eversion (or pronation), in which the sole is tipped out, and ankle inversion (or supination), in which the sole of the foot is tipped in.

ANKLE JOINT—MAIN MUSCLES:
- The anterior tibialis attaches to the knee and ankle and runs along the face of the tibia.
- The gastrocnemius is a big muscle in the calf that joins at the ankle and becomes the Achilles tendon.
- The soleus is beneath the gastrocnemius.
- The posterior tibialis lies deep in the back of the leg.
- The extensor digitorum longus lies in the front of the leg.
- The peroneal muscles (peroneus tertius, peroneus longus, and peroneus brevis) are deep inside the lower leg.

ANKLE JOINT—MAIN MOVEMENTS OF MUSCLES:
- The anterior tibialis is involved in flexing the foot and toes back and tipping the sole of the foot in.
- The gastrocnemius is involved in curling the foot and toes downward (ankle plantar flexion).
- The soleus is involved in curling the foot and toes downward.
- The posterior tibialis is involved in tipping the sole of the foot in while the foot is curled down in plantar flexion.
- The extensor digitorum longus is involved in flexing the foot and tipping the sole of the foot out.
- The peroneal muscles are involved in tipping the sole of the foot out. The peroneus tertius is also involved in flexing the foot and toes.

MUSCULAR SYSTEM – Key Points

Classification
A muscle cell not only has the ability to propagate an action potential along its cell membrane, as does a nerve cell, but also has the internal machinery to give it the unique ability to contract.

Most muscles in the body can be classified as striated muscles in reference to the fact that when observed under a light microscope the muscular tissue has light and dark bands or striations running across it. Although both skeletal and cardiac muscles are striated and therefore have similar structural organizations, they do possess some characteristic functional differences.

In contrast to skeletal muscle, cardiac muscle is a functional syncytium. This means that although anatomically it consists of individual cells the entire mass normally responds as a unit and all of the cells contract together. In addition, cardiac muscle has the property of automaticity which means that the heart initiates its own contraction without the need for motor nerves.

Non-striated muscle consists of multi-unit and unitary (visceral) smooth muscle. Visceral smooth muscle has many of the properties of cardiac muscle. To some extent it acts as a functional syncytium (e.g., areas of intestinal smooth muscle will contract as a unit. Smooth muscle is part of the urinary bladder, uterus, spleen, gallbladder, and numerous other internal organs. It is also the muscle of blood vessels, respiratory tracts, and the iris of the eye.

Skeletal Muscles
In order for the human being to carry out the many intricate movements that must be performed, approximately 650 skeletal muscles of various lengths, shapes, and strength play a part. Each muscle consists of many muscle cells or fibers held together and surrounded by connective tissue that gives functional integrity to the system. Three definite units are commonly referred to:

(1) endomysium—connective tissue layer enveloping a single fiber;
(2) perimysium—connective tissue layer enveloping a bundle of fibers;
(3) epimysium—connective tissue layer enveloping the entire muscle

Muscle Attachment and Function
For coordinated movement to take place, the muscle must attach to either bone or cartilage or, as in the case of the muscles of facial expression, to skin. The portion of a muscle attaching to bone is the tendon. A muscle has two extremities, its origin and its insertion.

Structural Organization of a Muscle Fiber
A muscle fiber is a single muscle cell. If we look at a section of a fiber we see that it is complete with a cell membrane called the sarcolemma and has several nuclei located just under the sarcolemma—it is multinucleated. Each fiber is composed of numerous cylindrical fibrils running the entire length of the fiber.

Myofilaments
The thick and thin myofilaments form the contractile machinery of muscle and are made up of proteins. Approximately 54% of all the contractile proteins (by weight) is myosin. The thick myofilament is composed of many myosin molecules oriented tail-end to tail-end at the center

- 59 -

with myosin molecules staggered from the center to the myofilament tip. The second major contractile protein is actin. Actin is a globular protein.

Sarcoplasm
The sarcoplasm (cytoplasm of the muscle cell) contains Golgi complexes near the nuclei. Mitochondria are found between the myogibrils and just below the sarcolemma. The myofibrils are surrounded by smooth endoplasmic reticulum (*sarcoplasmic reticulum*) composed of a longitudinally arranged tubular network (*sarcotubules*).

The complex (terminal cistern-T tubule-terminal cistern) formed at this position is known as a *triad*. The T tubules function to bring a wave of depolarization of the sarcolemma into the fiber and thus into intimate relationship with the terminal cisternae.

Excitation
Contraction in a skeletal muscle is triggered by the generation of an action potential in the muscle membrane. Each motor neuron upon entering a skeletal muscle loses its myelin sheath and divides into branches with each branch innervating a single muscle fiber, forming a *neuromuscular junction*. Each fiber normally has one neuromuscular junction which is located near the center of the fiber. A *motor unit* consists of a single motor neuron and all the muscle fibers innervated by it. The *motor end plate* is the specialized part of the muscle fiber's membrane lying under the neuron.

Contraction

According to the sliding filament theory (Huxley) the sacromere response to excitation involves the sliding of thin and thick myofilaments past one another making and breaking chemical bonds with each other as they go. Neither the thick nor thin myofilaments change in length. If we could imagine observing this contraction under a light microscope we would see the narrowing of the "H" and "I" bands during contraction while the width of the "A" band would remain constant.

Muscle Twitch
A muscle's response to a single maximal stimulus is a *muscle twitch*. The beginning of muscular activity is signaled by the record of the *electrical activity* in the sarcolemma. The *latent period* is the delay between imposition of the stimulus and the development of tension.

Tetanus
When a volley of stimuli is applied to a muscle, each succeeding stimulus may arrive before the muscle can completely relax from the contraction caused by the preceding stimulus. The result is *summation*, an increased strength of contraction. If the frequency of stimulation is very fast, individual contractions fuse and the muscle smoothly and fully contracts. This is a *tetanus*.

Energy Sources
In any phenomenon including muscular contraction the energy input to the system and the energy output from the system are equal. Let us consider first the energy sources for muscular contraction. The immediate energy source for contraction is ATP which can be hydrolyzed by actomyosin to give ADP, P_i, and the energy which is in some way associated with cross-bridge motion.

Types of Muscle Fibers

Skeletal muscle fibers can be described, on the bases of structure and function, as follows:

1. *White (fast) fibers* – contract rapidly; fatigue quickly; energy production is mainly via anaerobic glycolysis; contain relatively few mitochondria; examples are the muscles of the eye.
2. *Red (slow) fibers* – contract slowly; fatigue slowly; energy production is mainly via oxidative phosphorylation (aerobic); contain relatively many mitochondria; examples are postural muscles.
3. *Intermediate fibers* – have structural and functional qualities between those of white and of red fibers.

MUSCLES—TYPES; PLANES OF MOVEMENT; ACTION

SLOW TWITCH MUSCLE FIBERS and FAST TWITCH MUSCLE FIBERS:
Slow twitch fibers (ST or Type I) can work longer without tiring. Slow twitch fibers have many mitochondria in the cells, make ATP energy with oxygen, and are used primarily for activities involving moderate force that last a long time. Fast twitch fibers (FT or Type II) work for shorter times and tire easily, make ATP energy without oxygen, and are better used for short, forceful activities. There are two types of fast twitch fibers, type a and b. Fast twitch a (or Type IIa) fibers can make energy with or without oxygen, while fast twitch b (or type IIb) fibers are only used in the fastest and most intense activities and can only make energy without oxygen. Most muscles have both fast twitch and slow twitch muscles, but the percentage of each type will vary depending on the role of the muscle in the body.

THREE CARDINAL PLANES OF MOVEMENT; FLEXION, EXTENSION, ABDUCTION, ADDUCTION, ROTATION, and CIRCUMDUCTION:
The cardinal planes of movement are three imaginary surfaces which run through the body in order to explain a motion. The **horizontal plane** (also called the transverse plane) separates the body into top and bottom parts. The **frontal plane** separates the body into front and back parts. The **saggital plane** separates the body into left and right parts. **Flexion** is a motion of a joint which folds or curls the adjoining bones closer together (such as a bicep curl). **Extension** is the opposite of flexion, in which a bent joint unfolds to separate the two adjoining bones. **Abduction** is any motion that goes away from the center of the body. **Adduction** is any motion that goes toward the center of the body. **Rotation** is a motion that moves around one point or plane. **Circumduction** is any motion that involves an arm or leg creating a circle.

FUNCTION/ROLE OF DIFFERENT MUSCLE TYPES IN BODY MOVEMENT:
An **agonist**, or "prime mover," is the muscle that contracts to make the motion happen. An **antagonist** is the opposing muscle that stretches to allow the agonist to shorten and create motion. An **assistor** is a muscle that helps a motion, but is not primarily responsible for the motion. It may also be called the secondary mover. A **stabilizer** is a muscle that holds a steady tightness. The contracting muscle might not move much at all, but may keep the surrounding muscles still so that another set of muscles might move. A **synergist** is a muscle that works with the agonist in a mutually beneficial way.

MAIN ACTION OF MUSCLES:

An *isometric action* is stable and unmoving. The joint does not move and the muscle does not change in length. Isometric exercise will result in added strength only in the exact position the action was held. An *isokinetic action* is a motion made on a machine that controls the speed and force of the movement. An *isotonic (dynamic) action* moves visibly, and is the action most often associated with standard muscle training. The two types of isotonic actions are:

1. Concentric action (or positive contraction), which is a motion of the muscle as it works against a resistance that results in a shorter muscle

2. Eccentric action (or negative contraction), which is a motion of the muscle as it lengthens against a resistance.

THREE TYPES OF MUSCLE:

1. Smooth muscle is smooth in appearance and works without conscious thought. It is usually found in the organs of the body.

2. Cardiac muscle is the muscle of the heart. The fibers work without conscious thought and tighten in unison.

3. Skeletal muscle (also called striated muscle) is controlled with intent and contracts to move the bones and joints.

There are *four arrangements* for skeletal muscles:

1. *Fusiform* muscle is arranged along the same direction as the resistance, in a long thin shape with the ends narrower than the body of the muscle.
2. *Longitudinal* muscle is long and flat.
3. *Fan-shaped* muscle (also called triangular muscle) is flat and spreads out from a smaller point to a wide end.
4. *Pennate* muscle is dense muscle with the fibers arranged diagonally from the direction of the resistance and may look like a feather.

GENERAL PRINCIPLES; DEFINITIONS; ELEMENTS OF TRAINING

GENERAL EXERCISE PRINCIPLES:

1. Give verbal cues or directions during exercise.
2. Recognize substitution with abnormal movement.
3. Modify the parameters to fit the activity.
4. Specify your goals from the exercise.
5. Start at the level determined by the evaluation.
6. Base your activities upon your assessment.
7. Demonstrate the exercise you want the client to perform.
8. Position the client in a safe position.
9. Make sure all joints are in proper position.

WARM-UP and COOL-DOWN (IMPORTANCE TO EXERCISE PROGRAM):

Warm-up is a short (8-12 minute) period in which a person will stretch the big muscles of the body and move the body less vigorously than he will during the exercise so as to get the body ready to work. A good warm-up may be able to prevent injuries to muscles.

A *cool-down* is a very short (3-5 minute) time at the end of an exercise period in which the person starts slowing down his or her activity. This lets the blood pressure and circulation normalize and thus helps to prevent dizziness. At the end of the cool-down, the person may choose to stretch the muscles that were used in the exercise in order to possibly reduce muscle soreness.

FLEXIBILITY—DEFINITION; BENEFITS PRACTICING FLEXIBILITY ACTIVITIES:

Flexibility is how far a person can move the joints. This ability depends on how far the muscles and connecting tissues can stretch easily, and each joint and joint action will have independent flexibility so that the ability to stretch in one way will not necessarily mean that the person will be able to stretch another way or another area similarly. Flexibility also means how long each muscle and connecting tissue group is when the joint is not moving. Longer muscles mean more flexibility.

- ✓ Fewer injuries
- ✓ less muscle tightness
- ✓ less discomfort of the muscles, particularly the back
- ✓ better spinal alignment
- ✓ better ability to react to stimuli
- ✓ lower levels of stress
- ✓ better awareness of the body
- ✓ better capability to do normal tasks

FLEXIBILITY—GUIDELINES SET BY AMERICAN COLLEGE OF SPORTS MEDICINE; MUSCLES THAT ARE FREQUENTLY TOO TIGHT:

- ✓ The muscles should be warmed up before beginning a stretching activity.
- ✓ Start with the biggest muscle groups, do stretches steadily and hold in one position for 15-30 seconds.
- ✓ Pay close attention to any muscle groups that may be especially inflexible or do not permit much movement.
- ✓ Stretching shows results only in the short-term, so doing flexibility exercises daily, or at least 2-3 times a week, will reveal the most benefits. Flexibility will be reduced if not practiced frequently.
- ✓ When doing a stretch, move just until the muscle is tense, but not painful.
- ✓ Repeat each stretch 2-4 times.
- ✓ Over time, increase the amount of stretch in order to see improvement.
- ✓ The upper trapezius, pectoralis major, anterior deltoid, erector spinae (the part in the lumbar spine), iliopsoas, hamstrings, gastrocnemius and soleus are often tight in most people.

MYOFASCIAL RELEASE; LIGAMENT LAXITY:

In myofascial release, the person uses a foam roller to rub an area that is tight and inflexible. This will release the tightness of the tissues surrounding a muscle that may be preventing the muscle joint from reaching its full motion. The tight area is placed over the roller and moved back and forth. When a particularly tense area is reached, the roller is held against the spot for several seconds to let the tissues loosen up. Ligament laxity (sometimes called "double jointedness") is when a person has genetically longer ligaments, thus allowing the joints to be more flexible than they would otherwise be. These people are more prone to injury because of their ability to be able to move into unusual positions.

CARDIORESPIRATORY FITNESS PROGRAMS—DURATION and FREQUENCY:

Duration is the length of time an exercise is maintained. The American College of Sports Medicine (ACSM) recommends a total of 20-60 minutes of aerobic activity each day, which can be accumulated in 10-minute periods throughout a day or all at one time. With increased duration of exercise, intensity can be reduced and results will still be seen.

Frequency is the number of days per week a person exercises. The ACSM recommends a person exercise 3-5 times per week. Clients who are trying to lose body fat should increase their frequency so as to use more calories. However, exercising more than 5 days per week has not been shown to improve fitness and could increase the likelihood of injury.

CARDIOVASCULAR TRAINING—OVERLOAD, INTENSITY, SPECIFICITY, MODE, DURATION, FREQUENCY:

Overload is the concept of working the body harder, longer, more frequently, or in a different way than it has in the past to increase the efficiency of the cardiovascular system.
Intensity is how hard an activity is done. *Specificity* is the concept that practicing an activity will result in improvement in only that particular activity. It is also called "SAID" (specific adaptations to imposed demands). *Mode* is the kind of exercise that a person does in order to improve the efficiency of the heart, blood vessels and lungs. *Duration* is the length of time an activity is performed. *Frequency* is the number of times (usually measured per week) that an activity is performed.

HEART, LUNGS and BLOOD VESSELS—GUIDELINES for IMPROVING EFFICIENCY (AMERICAN COLLEGE OF SPORTS MEDICINE):

- *Kind of exercise:* exercises in which bigger muscles are used for an uninterrupted time, and the heart rate is increased.
- *How often:* exercise at least 3 days out of each week. More than 5 days of exercise may not show any improvement.
- *How hard:* exercise at a level in which the heart rate is at 40 to 85% of the HRR (subtract the resting heart rate from the estimated maximum rate the heart will beat). Less fit people should aim for the lower target. Another option is to exercise at 64 – 94% of the estimated maximum rate the heart will beat.
- *How long:* at least 20 minutes per day of exercise, although up to an hour is preferable. Exercise can be in shorter intervals accrued during one day.
- The exercise should also increase over time in how hard it is, and how often and for how long it is performed.

CONTINUOUS TRAINING and INTERVAL TRAINING:

Continuous training is a routine for improving the efficiency of the heart, lungs and blood vessels by exercising for a long time without resting and at a consistent level of vigor. This may become monotonous for the person exercising, but is simple to learn. *Interval training* is a routine for improving the efficiency of the heart, lungs and blood vessels by alternating highly vigorous activity with less vigorous activity during one exercise session. This may be more engaging to the person so that they are more likely to continue with it, and it is easy to increase the level of vigor or the length of time the exercise is performed as fitness is improved.

FARTLEK TRAINING, SUPER CIRCUIT TRAINING and CROSS-TRAINING:

Fartlek training is a more spontaneous version of interval training in which the person switches between more vigorous activity and less vigorous activity. It is also called speed play training and was developed for running programs, but can be applied to any other cardiovascular fitness activity. *Super circuit training* is a routine for improving the efficiency of the heart, lungs and blood vessels. It involves switching between vigorous aerobic exercise and weight training activities in order to gain muscle fitness and cardiovascular fitness. *Cross-training* is a routine for improving the efficiency of the heart, lungs and blood vessels involving practicing a variety of activities over time (either in one session, over one week, or over a year) in order to improve performance in different areas, as well as reduce the rate of injury and increase fitness over a greater range of muscles.

PROGRESSION—THE THREE STAGES:
Progression is the concept of increasing the level of activity through three stages in order to eventually reach the point when the person sustains a satisfactory level of fitness over time. The **initial conditioning stage** is when a person begins exercising. Exercise programs at this stage should be attainable and motivating, and include a significant period of warming up the muscles, lower intensity activities and a significant period of cooling down the muscles. Exercise may initially be scheduled for as little as 12 minutes, 3 days per week, with an increase over time. The **improvement stage** is the stage in which the person is well motivated by the initial success. Exercise should increase in how hard it is, and how long and how often it is performed. The **maintenance stage** is the final stage when the person begins to sustain fitness over time.

MUSCULAR FITNESS—DEFINITION; ADVANTAGES:
Muscular fitness is a stage at which the muscle operates efficiently and easily, with increased force and the ability to work for long periods of time. It is the muscle's response to training.
- The body is capable of moving easier and with better efficiency.
- Bones are denser and less likely to develop osteoporosis.
- Insurance against losing muscle as the body ages
- Possible increase in energy usage so that less fat is stored (this may or may not be true, as studies are unclear).
- Tendons and ligaments are stronger and may be less prone to injury
- Better ability to carry out various specific muscle tasks
- The person may begin to feel better about himself and his life.

Some muscle training programs such as circuit weight training can result in improved functioning of the lungs, heart, blood vessels and energy metabolism.

MUSCULAR STRENGTH, MUSCULAR ENDURANCE, MUSCLE POWER, MUSCLE STABILITY, MUSCLE HYPERTROPHY and VOLUME:
Muscular strength is how hard a muscle can move at once. **Muscular endurance** is how many times a muscle can do a movement or how long a stationary position can be held. **Muscle power** is a combination of muscle strength and the speed at which the movement can be done. **Muscle stability** is how well a muscle can hold still, which is especially important for abdominal and back muscles involved in standing. **Muscle hypertrophy** is a muscle getting larger as it is trained. **Volume** is the number of times a movement is done ("repetitions") multiplied by the amount of force being moved.

MUSCLE TRAINING PLAN—GUIDELINES OF AMERICAN COLLEGE OF SPORTS MEDICINE:
- ✓ Work one group of an activity until exhausted but still able to do the exercise correctly.
- ✓ Do each activity 8-12 times.
- ✓ Control the forward and reverse motions of the activity in a deliberate way.
- ✓ All muscle groups should be exercised 2-3 times each week, but any particular muscle group should not be worked on successive days (rest days are important to muscle fitness and to avoid injury). In addition, try to do a variety of activities for each muscle group.
- ✓ A total muscle training plan should include at least 8 activities, working all the biggest muscle groups of the body rather than concentrating on just one or two muscle groups.

MUSCLE TRAINING—SETS, REPETITIONS AND INTENSITY:

A set is doing an activity several times in a row. A single-set program involves repeating the activity until the muscles are too exhausted to continue doing the activity correctly. A multi-set program involves repeating the exercise until the muscle begins to get tired, and then resting for a few minutes, then doing a second set. Both methods have been shown to have similar results. *Repetitions* are the number of times an activity is repeated in each session. Programs considered high-intensity will include a number of repetitions that result in the muscle becoming so tired that it will no longer do the exercise (the muscle will recover in a few minutes). *Lower-intensity* programs involve doing enough repetitions to make the muscle tired but still able to work. *High-intensity* training may be more effective at increasing strength quickly.

MUSCLE TRAINING—FREQUENCY, VARIETY, ORDER OF EXERCISES AND PROGRESSION:

Muscles need rest from a workout, so 2-3 workouts per week with 2 days in between is recommended. To maintain a habit, different muscle groups can be worked on different days with rest for the worked muscle groups. Varying the activities is important for verifying that all muscles are worked, and to provide a more interesting workout, thus reducing the likelihood of boredom or dropping out of the program. The biggest muscle groups are involved in many different movements for different parts of the body, so it is recommended that the biggest muscle groups be worked first. Activities that work multiple muscle groups should be done before activities that work only one group. However, the back and torso muscles will be needed in most other activities and should not be worked too hard early in the program, otherwise other activities will be difficult to perform.

MUSCLE TRAINING—PROGRESSION AND SPEED:

Muscles will adjust to the workload they are given, so over time the workload must increase in order for muscles to continue to become stronger. This is referred to as progressive resistance exercise (PRE). In a double-progressive program, the number of times the activity is repeated is increased over time until the person can perform the activity 12 or more times without difficulty, and then weight is added, the number of repetitions is decreased and the process begins again. Additionally, more challenging activities can be added to the workout in order to capitalize on the person's increasing muscular fitness.

Speed is another way that progression can be used. Performing an activity very fast should be reserved for more experienced people, however. Most people should perform muscle training exercises slowly and deliberately.

FUNCTIONAL TRAINING; CLOSED KINETIC CHAIN EXERCISE (CKC); OPEN KINETIC CHAIN EXERCISE (OKC):

Functional training means developing a muscle fitness program that improves the ability to perform normal daily tasks. *Closed kinetic chain exercises* (CKC) are activities that are similar to actions performed in the life of an average person. These activities are usually done with the feet on the floor. *Open kinetic chain exercises* (OKC) are activities that segregate muscle groups in a way that is not typical for daily tasks. Often machines are used for these types of activities. Most people who are not athletes should do more closed kinetic chain exercises. Senior citizens and unfit people will benefit the most from this type of functional training.

PYRAMID SYSTEM; SUPER-SLOW TRAINING SYSTEM; CHEAT SYSTEM OF TRAINING:

The *pyramid system* involves increasing or decreasing weights and repetitions in one training session. An ascending pyramid system involves lifting more weight while decreasing the number of times the weight is lifted. A descending pyramid involves starting with the most weight the person can lift one time, and then lifting less weight more times with each set. The complete pyramid system is a combination of these two systems, lifting more weight fewer times until the person reaches his maximum weight, and then lifting less weight more times. **Super-slow training** involves doing an activity very slowly, pausing at the peak of the resistance, and then returning very slowly. The **cheat system** involves doing an activity correctly until the muscles are completely exhausted, then doing the activity incorrectly a few more times, allowing gravity or other muscles to complete the activity. This has a high risk of injury.

PRE-EXAHAUSTION SYSTEM; PRIORITY TRAINING; SPLIT ROUTINE SYSTEM; BLITZ SYSTEM:

The **pre-exhaustion system** involves doing activities that use bigger muscle sets before activities that use big and small muscle sets. Smaller muscles will tire before bigger muscles, so if the bigger muscles are not somewhat tired before doing the combined activity, the person will have to stop lifting when the smaller muscles get tired and the bigger muscles will not work to their maximum capacity. If the muscles do not work to maximum capacity, they cannot be overloaded, and improvements in strength are not likely. **Priority training** focuses on working smaller, less strong muscles at the beginning of an exercise session. The **split routine system** alternates working muscle groups on different days so that the person works out every day, but some muscles will rest on any given day. The **blitz system** is similar to a split routine, but each session focuses on only one particular part of the body.

CIRCUIT TRAINING, SUPER-CIRCUIT TRAINING, PARTIAL REPETITIONS, FORCED REPETITIONS, ECCENTRIC TRAINING:

Circuit training involves moving from one activity to another without a break. The person does one set of each activity with moderate vigor. **Super-circuit training** involves alternating weight training with cardiovascular exercises. The **partial repetitions** system (or "burn system") involves the person working as hard as she can in complete motion activities, then doing variations of those activities while only partially completing the movement. The **forced repetitions** system involves the person working as hard as she can on an activity, then a trainer steps in to help her repeat the activity a few more times. **Eccentric training** (or "negative training") involves working opposing muscle groups harder. Either a special machine increases the weight on the return (eccentric) part of the activity, or the trainer will help the person lift the weight on the main part of the activity, then let go for the return part.

Circuit Training

Circuit training is a type of training that comprises a series of 4 to 10 exercises, with brief rest intervals between each exercise. Circuit training stresses the musculoskeletal system resulting in muscle endurance and cardiovascular adaptations occurring. Circuit training is an excellent alternative to more specific sport related training.

Circuit training provides for a more general conditioning to improve on various aspects of the player's conditioning. Improving body composition, muscle strength and endurance and cardiovascular fitness. All the essential aspects that an athlete needs to optimise performance.

A positive aspect of circuit training is that it is versatile. It can be used as either a power-based training session (short time periods, longer rests, and high intensity) or as an endurance-based session (longer time periods, less rest, high intensity).

Detraining

Short-term detraining (five weeks) induces significant changes in the metabolic response to exercise, with decreased fat breakdown during exercise and increased reliance on glucose.

However, long-term detraining produces more significant and dramatic changes, with lower fatty acid availability giving rise to an even higher reliance on glucose during exercise. Additionally, destruction of red blood cells (haemolysis) may be observed during exercise.

OVERTRAINING, DETRAINING AND RETRAINING:

Overtraining is when the body loses the ability to do an activity as well as it could, even though the person continues to exercise. Injuries may be increased. This is the result of too much exercise and too little rest. Emotional problems can also appear with overtraining. **Detraining** is when the body loses its ability to do an activity because the person has stopped exercising. Muscles lose the ability to lift as much weight as they could and begin to shrink. The ability to use muscles or participate in long-term aerobic activities will also be lessened. **Retraining** is the process of improving one's fitness level after an interval of not exercising. A person who exercises a lot will lose more performance ability when he stops exercising than will a person who is less active.

RESISTANCE TRAINING EQUIPMENT—THREE TYPES; ADVANTAGES and DISADVANTAGES:

Dynamic constant resistance equipment, such as free weights, keep the weight the same during the entire movement. This equipment is uncomplicated, economical, and the movements mimic the motions used in daily activities. They are also more likely to cause injury. **Dynamic variable** resistance equipment vary the force so that the weight is heavier at the angle in the movement that the muscle should be the strongest. Machines used in weight rooms that use pulleys or other apparatus to help the user through the movement are examples of this equipment. These are not dangerous to use and simple to learn, but the cost may be prohibitive. **Isokinetic resistance** equipment keeps the weight and speed the same during the entire movement. Physical therapists often use these for patient therapies. These are not likely to cause injury, but only work one muscle group and might be difficult to gain access to.

ISOMETRIC (STATIC) RESISTANCE TRAINING, CORE EXERCISE, CORE TRAINING, BALANCE, and PLYOMETRIC TRAINING:

Isometric resistance training is a way of developing muscle in which the muscle is held against a force in one position without moving. The most improvements in the muscle performance will be when the muscle is in the position that the training was done. Proper breathing is essential in this type of training. A **core exercise** is one that uses more than one muscle group and joint, such as squats. **Core training** is a program of exercise in which the muscles of the abdomen and back are the focus. Focusing also on muscles that attach to the torso will help to prevent injury. **Balance** is being able to stay in one place for an extended time. **Plyometric training** is a program of exercise in which a resistance is combined with a quick movement, thereby combining strength training with speed development.

PERIODIZATION and PLATEAU (how to overcome); SUPER-SET SYSTEM, TRI-SET, GIANT SET:

Periodization means changing the exercise plan over time. This can avoid boredom and can work muscles that have been neglected in previous programs. A **plateau** is when a muscle seems to stop improving and stays at the same level of strength despite continued attempts at training. To resume improvement, add different activities to the program, rest for longer periods of time, work at different intensities, change the number of times the exercise is done, or choose a different method of training. A **super-set system** is doing two activities, one right after the other, with no recovery period in between. This can be done with the same or different sets of muscles. The **tri-set system** is doing three activities with no recovery period in between. Usually tri-set systems will work the same set of muscles.

A **giant set** is doing four or more activities with no recovery time in between.

PERIODIZATION:

Periodization is the gradual cycling of specificity, intensity, and volume of training to achieve peak levels of strength. The cycle will shift gradually from high volume and low intensity to low volume high intensity over several weeks. The length of the cycle revolves around the dates of competition. The typical powerlifting cycle will consist of three phases: Hypertrophy, Strength, and Power.

The first phase is the hypertrophy phase, hypertrophy, will normally consist of eight to ten repetitions per set. This phase may last from one to six weeks with intensities from 65% to 79% of one repetition maximum (1 RM). The hypertrophy phase is responsible for developing a good muscular and metabolic base for the future. All rest between sets in this phase should be kept between 45 seconds and 1.5 minutes. Shorter rests in this phase will maximize the natural primary anabolic hormones involved in muscle tissue growth such as testosterone, growth hormone, and insulinlike growth factors, while minimizing cortisol production.

The second phase is called the strength phase. It will normally consist of five to eight repetitions per set. This phase may last from two to eight weeks. In the strength phase the weight intensity is gradually increased to loads of 80% to 90% of 1 RM. Obviously this is the phase where the athlete increases muscular strength. The rest between stets in the strength phase should be increased to about five minutes. This length of time will assure that the muscles have completely recovered from the higher intensity workout.

The final phase of the powerlifting cycle is the power phase. This phase will consist of sets with repetitions of one to four and intensity levels gradually increasing from 90% to 107% of 1 RM. The power phase is where the athlete peaks the strength levels for competition. Rest between sets in the power phase should be increased to about five to ten minutes. These maximal to near maximal repetitions require much more time for the muscle to recover 100% and be ready for the next set.

BREATHING EXERCISES

Breathing exercises help clients recover during a strength training program. The following is a list of key breathing techniques.

Diaphragmatic Breathing
Sit comfortably upright in a chair with your feet slightly apart and hands resting in your lap or palms down on your knees.
Inhale slowly and deeply through your nose.
Feel your stomach expand as your lungs fill with air.

Purse Lip Beathing
Sit /stand upright comfortably with feet slightly apart.

Inhale slowly through the nose.
Purse lips slightly as if to whistle.
Exhale out slowly through the pursed lips. (Take 3-4 times longer than inhaling)
Do not force air out.

Natural Breathing
Sit /stand comfortably upright with feet slightly apart.
Inhale through your nose filling first the lower part of your lungs then the middle part, then the upper part.
Hold your breath for a few seconds.
Exhale slowly.
Relax your abdomen and chest.

STRETCHING EXERCISES

Stretching should never cause severe pain. It is not unusual to experience mild discomfort or a mild pulling sensation. Make sure that your client's have warmed up before attempting stretching exercises.

The two types of stretching techniques are dynamic or static.

Dynamic stretching is used in both the warm up and cool down periods of exercising. It involves repeated and gentle, movements that create mild tension, but should not be painful or exhaustive. The dynamic stretch can be specific to the sport such as swinging a bat or a golf club or a low-level activity like walking.

Static stretching is more effective during cool down. It involves slow, controlled stretching with held positions for 10-20 seconds while breathing normally. It is designed to increase flexibility and focus on tight muscles.

TYPES OF STRETCHING:
Ballistic stretching is a fast, moving stretching, in which the person bounces into the stretch. Because this type of stretching can activate the myotatic reflex, it can lead to tighter muscles and more injuries, and is thus not recommended for most people. Static stretching is slowly moving into a position in order to lengthen a muscle, and then holding that position for 15-30 seconds. This is considered the safest method of stretching. Active stretching (also called unassisted stretching) is when a person does a stretch by himself by contracting the opposite muscles in order to lengthen the target muscle. Passive stretching (also called assisted stretching) is when the muscles are stretched by either another person or a machine.

MYOTATIC REFLEX:
The myotatic reflex (also called the stretch reflex) is the muscle's response to being stretched. When a muscle gets longer, the muscle spindles send messages to the muscle via the spinal cord to tighten the muscle. The muscle spindle is located between the sarcomeres of the muscle, and works quickly to tighten a muscle when it senses any variations in the muscle length. When a muscle is stretched fast, the muscle spindle acts fast to tighten the muscle. If the lengthening is done slowly, the muscle spindle will adjust to the new length of the muscle and will not send a tightening response. The Golgi tendon organ (GTO) is located at the point where the muscle

meets the tendon and responds to the tightness of a muscle. In a reflex called the inverse myotatic reflex, the GTO relaxes a muscle that is overtight, superceding the work of the muscle spindles.

PROPRIOCEPTIVE NEUROMUSCULAR FACILITATION (PNF):
PNF is a way of stretching that uses the muscles' response to lengthening and tightness. When contracting a muscle very tightly, the Golgi tendon organs will relax the muscle. The muscle can then be moved into a new position. There are **three common versions** of the PNF:
- Hold-relax (HR) involves a helper holding the part that is to be stretched while the person pushes or pulls against the other person without moving the joint. The muscle will then relax and the helper can reposition the body part.
- Contract-relax (CR) involves the helper holding the muscle, and the person moving the joint in opposition to the helper. Once the muscle is relaxed, the part can be moved into the new position.
- Contract-relax, antagonist-contract (CRAC) involves tightening the muscle then relaxing it and tightening the opposing muscle, which will move the original muscle to a new position.

STRETCHING EXERCISES TO INCREASE FLEXIBILITY—PECTORALIS MAJOR AND ANTERIOR DELTOID; LATISSIMUS DORSI:
Pectoralis major and anterior deltoid:
The butterfly chest stretch involves putting the hands behind the head, pushing the chest out and pulling the arms back. The standing chest stretch involves standing with arms low behind the back, with hands holding each other or apart. The standing unilateral wall stretch involves standing with one hand holding a wall, then turning the body away so that the arm stays on the wall and the chest muscles are stretched.
Latissimus dorsi:
The arms reach forward lat stretch involves bending forward at the hip and tightening the torso while reaching one arm up and slightly over the. The opposite hand should be placed on the thigh. The unilateral side stretch for lats involves sitting upright while reaching one arm up and slightly over the head and bending sideways at the waist. The opposite hand should be placed on the thigh or the floor.

STRETCHING EXERCISES TO INCREASE FLEXIBILITY—TRAPEZIUS, RHOMBOID, POSTERIOR DELTOID (UPPER BACK AND NECK); and ANTERIOR DELTOID, MEDIAL DELTOID, POSTERIOR DELTOID:
For the trapezius, rhomboid, and posterior deltoid: The lateral flexion neck stretch involves tipping the head to one side and holding for up to 30 seconds. The cervical spinal flexion neck stretch involves tipping the head down with the chin near the chest. The upper back stretch involves sitting or standing and reaching the arms in front of the body, holding the hands together. Curl the back so that the shoulder blades move away from each other.
For the anterior deltoid, medial deltoid, and posterior deltoid: The deltoid stretch in front involves reaching one arm across the front of the body, pulling on the wrist with the other hand. Shoulders should stay low while the stretch is held. The deltoid stretch in back involves reaching one arm across the back, pulling the wrist with the opposite hand and keeping the shoulders low.

STRETCHING EXERCISES TO INCREASE FLEXIBILITY—TRICEPS AND BICEPS:
The triceps stretch with arm overhead involves reaching one arm up and over the head, bending the forearm to the back. The elbow points upward. The triceps stretch with arm in front

involves reaching one arm across the front of the body and grasping the other shoulder with the elbow bent. The opposite hand should hold the elbow and pull gently to stretch the triceps. **The biceps stretch** with arms behind involves pushing the arms straight behind the back with palms facing outward without bending the arms. The biceps stretch with arm in front involves reaching one arm straight out in front of the body with the elbow facing down and the opposite arm holding up the arm under the elbow.

STRETCHING EXERCISES TO INCREASE FLEXIBILITY—RECTUS ABDOMINIS:
The prone modified cobra stretch involves lying face down on the floor, with upper body pressed upward, supported by the forearms. Shoulders should be low. The supine pencil stretch involves lying on the back with arms straight over the head, stretching the arms and legs away from each other. The supine knee down twist involves lying on the back with arms out to the side, hips bent and knees together and to one side. The head should be turned toward the side opposite the knees. The seated knee to chest twist involves sitting upright with one leg straight out in front and the other bent and crossed over the straight knee with the foot on the floor. The bent knee should be held in the arms and pulled in toward the chest. Turn the head and body outward toward the side of the bent leg.

STRETCHING EXERCISES TO INCREASE FLEXIBILITY—ERECTOR SPINAE:
The supine double knee to chest stretch involves lying on the back with knees bent to the chest. The lower back should press to the floor as the arms pull the knees in, keeping the stretch for up to 30 seconds. The all-fours angry cat stretch involves holding the body on knees and hands facing the floor, then rounding the back so that the head and buttocks move down and the torso muscles are pulled up for up to 30 seconds. The standing angry cat stretch involves standing with the hands resting on the thighs, then curling the back so that the head moves forward and the torso muscles are tightened.

STRETCHING EXERCISES TO INCREASE FLEXIBILITY—HIP FLEXORS:
The standing hip flexor stretch involves standing with one foot in front and one foot behind the body. The knees bend slightly and the back heel is raised up as the pelvis is tucked in and the torso muscles tightened. One hand can rest on a chair for support. The runner's lunge involves pushing one leg far behind the body, bending the front leg and placing the fingers on the floor on either side of the front foot for support. The bent knee should stay behind the foot. Push the hips downward to feel a stretch in the hip of the back leg. The supine hip flexor stretch involves lying on the back with one knee bent and pulled toward the chest.

STRETCHING EXERCISES TO INCREASE FLEXIBILITY—GLUTEUS MAXIMUS:
The supine double knee to chest stretch involves lying on the back with knees bent to the chest. The lower back should press to the floor as the arms pull the knees in, keeping the stretch for up to 30 seconds. The seated knee to chest twist involves sitting upright with one leg straight out in front and the other bent and crossed over the straight knee with the foot on the floor. The bent knee should be held in the arms and pulled in toward the chest. Turn the head and body outward toward the side of the bent leg and keep the stretch for up to 30 seconds.

STRETCHING EXERCISES TO INCREASE FLEXIBILITY—QUADRICEPS:
The prone quadriceps stretch involves lying face down and bending one leg up and pulling the foot toward the body. The face is pressed into the floor and the neck is straight. The side-lying quadriceps stretch involves lying on one side on the floor, with the floor-side arm under the head. The ankle away from the floor is bent, and the same-side arm pulls the foot toward the body and keeps the stretch for up to 30 seconds.The standing quadriceps stretch involves

standing and bending one foot backward with the same-side hand pulling the foot into the body. If necessary, the person can hold a wall or a chair with the other hand for balance.

STRETCHING EXERCISES TO INCREASE FLEXIBILITY—HAMSTRINGS:
The standing hamstring stretch involves standing with the hips bent, with one leg on a chair in front of the body. The upper body is tipped toward the foot, with the same-side hand on the leg or chair for support. The leg standing on the floor should be slightly bent, and the torso muscles should be tight. The supine hamstring stretch involves lying on the back with one leg straight up in the air and the other leg bent with the foot on the floor. The hands should be behind the straight leg's upper or lower leg, but not behind the knee. The seated unilateral hamstring stretch involves sitting with one leg straight out in front and the other leg bent so that the foot is placed flat against the other inner thigh. Bend forward slightly at the hips, moving the upper body toward the straight leg.

STRETCHING EXERCISES TO INCREASE FLEXIBILITY—GLUTEUS MEDIUS and GLUTEUS MINIMUS:
The figure four stretch involves lying on the back with one leg bent at the hip at a right angle, and the knee bent at a right angle. The other leg is bent at the hip and knee so that the ankle is resting against the thigh of the first leg. Hold the first thigh and pull toward the upper body, stretching the crossed over leg. The side-lying abductor stretch involves lying on one side, with the head on the arm, lower leg bent out in front and the lower leg bent and pushed toward the back. The front (lower) thigh should be at a right angle to the torso. The top hip should be straight and the knee pressed toward the floor.

STRETCHING EXERCISES TO INCREASE FLEXIBILITY—HIP ADDUCTORS:
The seated straddle stretch involves sitting with the legs straight out in front and spread out wide. The back must stay straight. Bend forward at the hips, moving the torso toward the feet. Hands can be in front or behind to support the torso and keep the back straight. The standing side lunge stretch involves standing with feet apart, bending one knee and bending the body at the hips over the bent knee. The other leg will be straight and the toe raised to stretch the hips. The hands will support the upper body by leaning on the thigh of the bent leg. The back stays straight.

STRETCHING EXERCISES TO INCREASE FLEXIBILITY—GASTROCNEMIUS and the SOLEUS:
The standing calf stretch involves standing with one leg in front of the body and one leg behind with the toes of both feet facing forward. The front leg is bent and the back leg is straight. Both feet stay flat on the floor. The seated calf stretch involves sitting with one leg straight out in front, and the other leg bent so that the foot is on the inner thigh of the straight leg. Flex the foot so that the toes are up and come back toward the body. For more stretch, use a strap to pull the toes back toward the body. The standing soleus stretch involves standing in the same position as in the standing calf stretch. The only difference is that the back leg will be bent slightly so that the stretch will be felt in the Achilles tendon at the lower part of the calf.

STRETCHING EXERCISES TO INCREASE FLEXIBILITY—ANTERIOR TIBIALIS:
The standing shin stretch involves standing with one foot in front and one foot behind. The front knee is bent a little bit, and the back foot is pointed so the tops of the toes are on the floor. The back leg should be straight otherwise. Hold a chair for balance if necessary. The seated shin stretch involves sitting with both legs straight out in front and together. The back is straight and the torso muscles tightened, but the torso remains upright (the hips are bent at a right angle to

the torso). The toes are pointed so that the toes are angled away from the body. The hands are at the sides to keep the upright stance.

EXERCISE TECHNIQUE

PROPER LIFTING TECHNIQUE—KEY POINTS:
- Hold the item with the hands closed around the object (often a barbell), either with the palm facing up (supinated) or down (pronated).
- The body should be balanced to hold the weight, with the feet placed slightly apart (usually under the shoulders), hips facing forward, and bending low at the hips and knees instead of at the waist. Hips should stay above the knees and eyes should be looking forward.
- The muscles of the abdomen and legs should do most of the work to get the bar off of the floor, and the weight should be held near the body. Be careful to keep knees bent a little bit to maintain balance
- The movement from the center of the body to the shoulders should be steady and even.

WEIGHT-LIFTING LIMITS—HOW DETERMINED; REST PERIODS BETWEEN SETS:
Most people will try different weights until they find the weight at which they can repeat the activity about 8 times. If the weight can be lifted many more times or not quite 8 times, then the weight should be adjusted accordingly. Another method involves finding the most weight the person can lift one time (called maximal lift or 1RM) then find 75% of that weight. The person should be able to lift that weight about 10 times. Higher weights should be repeated fewer times and lower weights should be repeated more times. Activities that are more difficult, have more weight, or activities in which the person works until the muscle cannot lift any more will require at least 2 minutes rest before repeating a set or moving to a new activity. Activities that are less difficult may not require any rest or may only require a few seconds rest.

BENCH PRESS—MUSCLES USED; MOVEMENTS PERFORMED; COMMON PROBLEMS; TRAINER'S RESPONSIBILITY FOR SPOTTING:
The pectoralis major, anterior deltoid, and the coracobrachialis work to perform the action of the upper arms and shoulders moving closer to the chest as the weight is lifted (horizontal adduction). The triceps straighten the elbow joint (elbow extension).
The pectoralis minor and serratus anterior work to spread the shoulder blades apart (scapular protraction) as the weight is lifted. **Common problems** include dropping the weight too quickly, the hips moving upward during the lift, allowing the back to arch off the bench, wrists moving out of the stable straight position, letting the bar bounce off of the chest, or holding one's breath. **The trainer** should stand firmly on the floor, knees slightly bent, at the person's head, with hands touching (but not lifting) the bar in an underhand position as the bar is lifted and lowered. If the bar is particularly heavy, up to three spotters may be necessary.

BENCH PRESS—PROPER BODY POSITION:
The person should lie on his back on the bench, feet on the floor or on a step if necessary. The back should be flat against the bench or relaxed. Hands are in an overhand position on the bar, usually far apart, but to engage the triceps more the hands can be placed closer together. Arms are straight out to the sides with elbow bent at a 90 degree angle. The weight will be up at first, then lowered, then raised. As the weight is lifted, only the arms and shoulders should move, but the muscles of the torso should contract to keep the body still. As the elbows straighten, do not allow them to over extend past 180 degrees. Breathe out when lifting up and breathe in when lowering the weight.

BENCH PRESS—WAYS TO CHANGE ACTIVITY FOR INDIVIDUAL LEVEL OF FITNESS:

For *less fit people* or people with back problems, put the feet higher than the floor (they can be even with the bench) so that the back is straighter and pressed to the bench. For people who have had shoulder problems, bring the hands closer together on the bar so that the elbows are closer to the body instead of straight out to the side. A *more fit person* can give a final push at the peak of the press to pull apart the shoulder blades, then release the shoulder blades before lowering the bar. More fit people could do a bench press with two dumbbells lifted at the same time rather than one barbell. To train the core muscles, a more fit person can do a bench press on an exercise ball instead of a bench so that the muscles of the torso stabilize the body during the lift.

INCLINE PRESS and DECLINE PRESS—MUSCLES USED; MOVEMENTS PERFORMED:

For the *incline press*, similar to the bench press, the pectoralis major, anterior deltoid, medial deltoid and the coracobrachialis work to perform the action of the upper arms and shoulders moving closer to the chest as the weight is lifted (horizontal adduction), although if the bench is at a very large tilt upward, the arms and shoulders may move farther up and away from the chest (shoulder abduction). In a *decline press*, the latissimus dorsi, teres major and sternal part of the pectorals are used to move the shoulders closer to the chest as the weight is lifted. If a person is very fit, the weight can be lowered so that the shoulder blades are pressed together, involving the pectoralis minor and lower trapezius.

DUMBBELL FLY—MUSCLES USED; MOVEMENTS PERFORMED; COMMON PROBLEMS; TRAINER'S RESPONSIBILITY FOR SPOTTING:

Similar to the bench press and incline press, the pectoralis major, anterior deltoid and coracobrachialis work to perform the action of the upper arms and shoulders moving closer to the chest as the weight is lifted (horizontal adduction). For fit people, the pectoralis minor and serratus anterior can be used to move the shoulder blades apart (protraction) at the peak of the lift. The subscapularis and teres major may be used to rotate the upper arm in toward the chest. *Common problems* include dropping the weights too fast, arching the back, and straining the chest muscles or the wrists moving out of the straight position.
The trainer should hold her hands near the wrists and forearms as the weights are raised and lowered. Depending on the height of the bench, the trainer may have to stand with knees bent or kneel on the floor at the person's head to spot the activity.

DUMBBELL FLY—PROPER BODY POSITION:

The person should lie flat on his back on a bench, with feet flat on the floor or elevated on a step. The back should be relaxed or pressed into the bench. The weights should be placed in the person's hands as is arms are extended up, with the palms facing inward as they hold the dumbbells. Elbows should be bent slightly. As the weights are lowered to the side, elbows should stay slightly bent, wrists should be straight, and the shoulder blades should be still. Only the shoulder joints should be moving the arms. Torso muscles and chest muscles should be tightened. The weights should not be dropped below the chest.

BILATERAL CABLE CROSS-OVER EXERCISE—MUSCLES USED; MOVEMENTS PERFORMED; COMMON PROBLEMS; TRAINER'S RESPONSIBILITY FOR SPOTTING:

Similar to the dumbbell fly, the pectoralis major, anterior deltoid and coracobrachialis work to move the upper arms and shoulders closer to the chest as the weight is lifted (horizontal adduction). For fit people, the pectoralis minor and serratus anterior are used to move the shoulder blades apart (protraction) at the peak of the lift. The subscapularis and teres major are used to rotate the upper arm in toward the chest. *Common problems* involve using too much

- 76 -

weight and having the pulleys yank the arms apart too quickly, thus pulling a muscle or tendon. If the weight is too high, the person might pull the torso back when pulling the arms in or forward when letting the arms return out. Wrists may also move out of the straight position. *The trainer* should stand behind the person and move her arms near the upper arms as the activity is performed.

BILATERAL CABLE CROSS-OVER EXERCISE—PROPER BODY POSITION:

The person should stand with hips spread apart or one foot slightly in front of the body and the other foot behind. Knees should be bent slightly, torso muscles tightened, and the shoulders lowered. Arms reach out to the sides to grasp the handles of the pulleys with the elbows bent slightly and palms facing forward. No other body part should move except the shoulder joint moving the arms. Pull the arms together against the resistance of the weights on the pulleys, with palms facing each other or turning downward. Slowly let the arms return to the original position, resisting against the weight without letting the pulleys yank the arms. The pulleys can also be adjusted to make the arms pull upward or downward as well.

PUSH-UP — MUSCLES USED; MOVEMENTS PERFORMED; COMMON PROBLEMS; TRAINER'S RESPONSIBILITY FOR SPOTTING:

The pectoralis major, anterior deltoid, and coracobrachialis move the upper arms and shoulders in toward the chest as the body is pushed upward (horizontal adduction). The triceps work to straighten the elbows. Some *common problems* encountered in the push-up are the hands moving away from a forward position, the torso muscles sagging downward, the hips pointing upward, not keeping the elbows slightly flexed at the peak of the press, moving the head and neck away from the straight position, or rolling the shoulder blades. *The trainer* should sit or kneel close to the person and may find it useful to place a hand under the abdominal muscles to remind the person to tighten them, or to hold the hands on the hips to remind the person to avoid tilting the hips upward.

PUSH-UP — PROPER BODY POSITION:

The person should be on the floor face down, hands flat on the floor with fingers pointed forward, arms mostly straight but slightly bent separated slightly wider than the shoulders and the body balanced evenly between the hands and either the toes or knees. The head and back should be in a straight line. The torso muscles should be tightened as the elbows bend to lower the upper body toward the floor. Do not allow the chest to touch the floor or rest on the floor but should stay about 3-5 inches above the floor at the lowest point. Eyes should point downward or just in front of the head. Then straighten the elbows to raise the chest upward.

PUSH-UP — WAYS TO CHANGE ACTIVITY FOR INDIVIDUAL LEVEL OF FITNESS:

The most standard change for the push-up for less fit people is to have the person balance the body on the knees instead of the toes, or to do the push-up against a wall or with the hands elevated on a bench. Additionally, the elbows can be kept closer to the body to avoid shoulder pain and reduce the workload on the shoulders. For more fit people, the person can do the push-up with the knees or feet elevated and the head down. In addition, the person can do a push-up with weights added onto his back, or the hands or feet placed on a shaky surface (such as a ball or roller) so that the core muscles of the abdomen must work harder. For extremely fit people, the push-up can be done explosively, pushing the body airborne and clapping the hands together at each peak (a plyometric variation).

REVERSE FLY—MUSCLES USED; MOVEMENTS PERFORMED; COMMON PROBLEMS; TRAINER'S RESPONSIBILITY FOR SPOTTING:

The posterior deltoid, infraspinatus and teres minor move the upper arms and shoulders to the side and away from the chest (horizontal abduction) and the trapezius III and the rhomboids move the shoulder blades together (retraction or adduction). **Common problems** involve using too much weight, which might result in shrugging the shoulder upward or straining the neck. Other problems include pushing the weight backwards instead of raising the arm up and to the side or not lifting the weight high enough to push the shoulder blades together. If the person is inclined face down, *the trainer* should be near the person's head with his arms closely following the movement of the person's arms as they lift. If the person is sitting or standing, *the trainer* should be behind the person, occasionally touching the shoulder blades to remind the person to pull them together.

REVERSE FLY—PROPER BODY POSITION:

The standard version involves a person lying face down on an inclined bench with the head up, and knee on the bench for stability. The person can also lie on a flat bench or sit bent forward at the hips. Arms should be down with palms facing inward. The head and neck should be in a straight line, and elbows bent slightly. The arms holding the dumbbells should be lifted straight out to the side of the body and slightly back to pull the shoulder blades together. Arms should not move down toward the hips or up toward the shoulders but should stay even with the chest. Once the weight has been lifted as high as possible, with the shoulder blades together, lower the arms slowly to the original position.

HORIZONTAL SEATED ROW—MUSCLES USED; MOVEMENTS PERFORMED; COMMON PROBLEMS; TRAINER'S RESPONSIBILITY FOR SPOTTING:

The posterior deltoid, infraspinatus, and teres minor are used for moving the upper arms out to the side from the front (horizontal abduction). The trapezius III and the rhomboids are used to pull the shoulder blades together (retraction), and the biceps, brachialis and brachioradialis are used to bend the elbows. **Common problems** involve moving the wrists from a straight position, or leaning the torso backwards to pull. Shrugging the shoulders also occurs with too much weight as does releasing the weight too quickly. **The trainer** should stand behind the person, touching the arms and shoulder blades as they move backward so as to direct them backwards and remind the person to pull the shoulder blades together.

HORIZONTAL SEATED ROW—PROPER BODY POSITION:

The person should sit at the pulley machine with the back straight, facing the pulley and weights, and with knees bent slightly and feet placed on the plates in front of the body. Hands should grab the bar with palms facing downward. Elbows should begin straight and arms are out in front. The torso muscles should be tightened as the elbows bend to pull the weight and the shoulder blades should come together. The bar should move toward the chest. The back and neck must be in a straight line, and the back should remain upright and not leaning backward. When releasing the weight, move slowly and do not let the pulley yank the arms. More fit people can do this activity on an exercise ball to better engage the muscles of the torso.

SHOULDER SHRUGS—MUSCLES USED; MOVEMENTS PERFORMED; PROPER BODY POSITION; COMMON PROBLEMS:

The trapezius I and II, rhomboids and levator scapulae are used to move the shoulder girdle up (elevation). The person should stand or sit with feet apart and the body balanced. Hold the dumbbells in each hand with palms facing inward. The back should be straight and in a line with the neck, and torso muscles should be tightened. Raise shoulders up, keeping arms straight and down. This is a very subtle movement. *Common problems* involve tension in the shoulders resulting in the person's shoulders being too often raised up, so they might have to focus more on lowering their shoulders to lengthen those muscles. The head might tip forward or backward during the exercise. Weights that are too heavy might result in the person swinging the arms or using the legs to move the weight up.

SCAPULAR DEPRESSION DIPS—MUSCLES USED; MOVEMENTS PERFORMED; COMMON PROBLEMS; TRAINER'S RESPONSIBILITY FOR SPOTTING; WAYS TO CHANGE ACTIVITY FOR INDIVIDUAL LEVEL OF FITNESS:

The trapezius IV and pectoralis minor move the shoulder blades downward. *Common problems* include tension in the wrists and either bending or overextending the elbows. Some people will swing the hips away from the bench during the movement, or will engage the legs to move the body instead of using the shoulders. *The trainer* should stand behind the person and touch the elbows and lower triceps so the client will not bend the elbows (as in triceps dips). If the client has wrist tension, move her hands more toward the edge of the bench so that the wrists are straighter. Less fit or less experienced people may do standard shoulder shrugs and dips from a standing position to learn how the motion feels. More fit people can do the activity on a dip stand, using all of the body's weight against the motion without the legs stabilizing the body.

SCAPULAR DEPRESSION DIPS—PROPER BODY POSITION:

The person stands to the side of a bench, with her back toward the bench. She should lower her body to rest her palms behind her on the bench with fingers curled over the edge of the bench and facing forward. Supporting herself with her palms, the person should keep her torso and neck straight, hips and knees bent and feet flat on the floor. The hips and buttocks will be just below the surface of the bench. The shoulders should begin in a shrug. Elbows will remain straight throughout the activity. Only the shoulders will move down out of the shrugged position as the body is lifted slightly, then the body is relaxed as the shoulders again lower into a shrug.

HIGH-PULLEY SCAPULAR DEPRESSION—MUSCLES USED; MOVEMENTS PERFORMED; PROPER BODY POSITION; COMMON PROBLEMS; TRAINER'S RESPONSIBILITY FOR SPOTTING:

The trapezius IV and pectoralis minor are used to move the shoulder blades down. The person should sit at the high-pulley cable column with arms up and holding the bar spaced widely apart, palms facing forward in an overhand grasp. Feet should be on the floor with the stabilizer placed on the thighs. The elbows should remain straight and only the shoulder blades should move as they pull down. This is a very subtle motion. *Common problems* involve overextending or bending the elbows, or pulling the torso backwards. *The trainer* should stand behind the person, using the outside of the hands to touch the shoulder blades so that the person can focus on the area being worked. If the person tries to bend the elbows as if doing a lat pull-down, hold the elbows straight.

FRONT RAISES—MUSCLES USED; MOVEMENTS PERFORMED; COMMON PROBLEMS; TRAINER'S RESPONSIBILITY FOR SPOTTING:

The anterior deltoid and pectoralis major work to lift the arms in front of the body (shoulder flexion). *Common problems* involve swaying the back and tipping the neck forward. The wrists may try to move out of a straight position. Knees may straighten or bend too much during the lift, and the person may try to shrug the shoulders to help with the lift. *The trainer* should stand behind the person with hands on the shoulders to remind the person to keep the shoulders low, but if the weights are particularly heavy, the trainer might need to stand in front and hold his hands under the weights to prevent the person from dropping them too quickly.

FRONT RAISES—PROPER BODY POSITION; WAYS TO CHANGE ACTIVITY FOR INDIVIDUAL LEVEL OF FITNESS:

The person begins by sitting or standing, feet apart for balance, arms down and palms facing down as they grasp the dumbbells. Shoulders are down and relaxed. If sitting, hips and knees should be bent, feet on the floor, and back and neck straight with torso muscles tightened. If standing, knees should be slightly bent for balance. Raise the arms holding the dumbbells up in front of the body, with palms facing downward. Arms should be lifted to just above shoulders. Shoulder blades should be kept low. Lower the arms slowly just as they were lifted. The seated position is best for less fit people, and anyone with back problems. If the person has shoulder problems, the lift can be done with the palms facing in. More fit people can try the activity on an exercise ball or standing with one leg raised.

LATERAL RAISES—MUSCLES USED; MOVEMENTS PERFORMED; PROPER BODY POSITION; TRAINER'S RESPONSIBILITY FOR SPOTTING:

The medial deltoid and supraspinatus move the shoulders and arms out away from the body (shoulder abduction), and the trapezius II, trapezius IV and serratus anterior are used for rotating the shoulder blades up. The person should stand holding dumbbells with arms to the side, palms facing in. The feet should be apart, balancing the body, with the knees bent a little. If seated, the hips and knees should be bent at right angles. Tighten the torso muscles and keep the shoulder blades lowered. Raise the arms up out to the sides no higher than the shoulders, keeping the palms facing down. The elbows should be the foremost part of the arm moving upward instead of the wrist. Lower arms slowly. **The trainer** should stand behind the person with hands near his arms or wrists, or possibly on the back as a reminder to keep the shoulder blades low.

LATERAL RAISES—FREQUENT PROBLEMS; WAYS TO CHANGE ACTIVITY FOR INDIVIDUAL LEVEL OF FITNESS:

With palms facing down (shoulders externally rotated), there is a possibility of injury to tendons in the shoulder. For this reason, less fit people might be encouraged to do the activity with palms facing forward instead. In addition, some possibility exists for injury to the lower back, so be sure the person had tightened the torso muscles and is standing upright. Very fit people may bend slightly at the hips to work the medial deltoid a little more. Many people will try to raise the shoulder blades or move the wrists out of a straight position. Less fit people could do the activity while seated or might try raising the weights only a third of the way up. More fit people may work one arm at a time, or sit on an exercise ball, stand on one foot or do leg raises while working the arms.

OVERHEAD PRESS—MUSCLES USED; MOVEMENTS PERFORMED; PROPER BODY POSITION:

The deltoids and supraspinatus are used to move the shoulders away from the body (abduction). The trapezius II, trapezius IV and serratus anterior are used to spin the shoulder blades up, and the triceps are used to straighten the elbows. The overhead press can be done while sitting or standing, with a barbell or with dumbbells. Either way, feet must be firmly planted, torso muscles tightened, and arms out to the sides with elbows bent at right angles. Palms should be facing in if using dumbbells, holding the bar in an overhand grip if using a barbell. Raise arms straight up while keeping shoulder blades low. Drop arms slowly. If using a barbell, be sure the bar is lowered in front of the head.

OVERHEAD PRESS—TRAINER'S RESPONSIBILITY FOR SPOTTING; FREQUENT PROBLEMS; WAYS TO CHANGE ACTIVITY FOR INDIVIDUAL LEVEL OF FITNESS:

- 80 -

The trainer should stand behind the person and hold hands under the person's arms or elbows. If a barbell is used, the trainer should hold his hands under the bar. Some people will remember doing this activity with a barbell behind the neck, but this may cause injury so encourage people to avoid that variation. Tipping the head forward is a common problem, and can also lead to injury. Less fit people should do this activity while seated. They can also lift the weights more in the front of the body than on the sides or try an incline bench. More fit people could try sitting on an exercise ball or on one leg, or can try doing the overhead press along with a lunge or squat.

UPRIGHT ROW—MUSCLES USED; MOVEMENTS PERFORMED; PROPER BODY POSITION; FREQUENT PROBLEMS:

The deltoids and supraspinatus move the shoulders up. The trapezius II, trapezius IV and serratus anterior spin the shoulder blades up. The biceps bend the elbows. While standing, place feet wide with toes facing forward. The arms will begin down, palms gripping the dumbbells or barbell and facing the body. The knees should be slightly bent, torso muscles tightened. Raise the bar in front of the body to chest height. The wrists should be relaxed and should not be doing the work, and should stay lower than the elbows. *Some frequent problems* include lifting the weight with the wrists. Some people might try to lift the weight over the shoulders, which could increase muscle development, but could also cause injury to the shoulder joint. If the weight is heavy, some people will tilt back when lifting.

EXTERNAL ROTATION WITH TUBE—MUSCLES USED; MOVEMENTS PERFORMED; PROPER BODY POSITION:

The infraspinatus and teres minor work to spin the shoulders out to the side, away from the body (external rotation). The person should stand or sit next to a machine with a pulley, or tie a rubber tube or band to a stable point. The arm that will be worked will be on the opposite side of the body from the machine or tube. The arm to be worked is bent at a right angle and the forearm reaches across the body to grip the handle of the pulley or tube. The palm of the hand may face in toward the body or up. The torso muscles should be tight. Pull the tube and spin the forearm, hand and wrist out from the body until they are pointed out to the side as far as possible. The elbow should stay close to the body. Return to original position slowly.

LAT PULL-DOWN — MUSCLES USED; MOVEMENTS PERFORMED; PROPER BODY POSITION; TRAINER'S RESPONSIBILITY FOR SPOTTING:

The latissmus dorsi, teres major and pectoralis major work to move the shoulders down and in (adduction). The pectoralis major and rhomboids work to spin the shoulder blades down. The biceps, brachialis and brachioradialis work to bend the elbows. The person should sit at a lat pull-down machine. The knees should be bent at right angles to the hips and the stabilizing bar positioned over the thighs. Grip the bar overhead with hands far apart and palms facing down. Tighten torso muscles and pull the bar down in front of the body, keeping shoulder blades low. Return to original position slowly and do not let the bar yank the arms. *The trainer* should hold her hands over the bar while standing behind the person.

LAT PULL-DOWN — FREQUENT PROBLEMS; WAYS TO CHANGE ACTIVITY FOR INDIVIDUAL LEVEL OF FITNESS:

Some *frequent problems* include tilting back to use the body weight to pull the bar down. Some people will want to do the back lat-row, which involves pulling the bar behind the head instead of in front. This version has been shown to be unsafe and increases the risk of injury so people should be discouraged from doing it. Some people, especially when working with weights that are too heavy, will let the machine yank the arms up, pulling the shoulder blades. This should also be discouraged, as it could lead to injury. People who have had shoulder problems should

- 81 -

not do this activity, but could try a low row. More fit people could do the activity while kneeling or on a high-pulley machine, letting them pull with each arm separately.

BENT-OVER ROW—MUSCLES USED; MOVEMENTS PERFORMED; TRAINER'S RESPONSIBILITY FOR SPOTTING; FREQUENT PROBLEMS; WAYS TO CHANGE ACTIVITY FOR INDIVIDUAL LEVEL OF FITNESS:

The latissimus dorsi, teres major, and pectoralis major work to move the arms down in front of the body (shoulder extension). The biceps, brachialis and brachioradialis work to bend the elbow. *The trainer* should stay near the working side with the hands near the weight, or on the back to remind the person to keep his back straight and the shoulder blades relaxed. *Frequent problems* include lowering the weight too abruptly, or tipping the head, curling the spine or hunching the shoulders when lifting the weight. Less fit people should instead consider a seated low row. More fit people could do this on a high-pulley machine and stand on one leg, or could stand instead of kneeling on the bench.

BENT-OVER ROW—PROPER BODY POSITION:

The person should place one knee on a bench and bend over, supporting the upper body with the arm on the same side on the bench. The opposite foot should be flat on the floor, and the back should be straight and parallel to the floor. The opposing arm (working arm) should hang down with the dumbbell, palm facing in toward the opposite arm. The torso muscles should be tight. Bend the elbow while lifting the weight so the upper arm becomes parallel with the back, but do not move the elbow away from the body or raise it any higher than the shoulder. Slowly return to the beginning position.

SEATED LAT (or LOW ROW)—MUSCLES USED; MOVEMENTS PERFORMED; PROPER BODY POSITION; FREQUENT PROBLEMS:

The latissimus dorsi and teres major work to lower the arms in front of the body (shoulder extension) and the biceps, brachialis and brachioradialis work to bend the elbows (elbow flexion). The person should be seated at a low pulley machine or a seated row machine. The knees should be bent slightly (or bent more if seated on or very close to the floor). The torso should be upright and perpendicular to the thighs, with the torso muscles tight. Arms should be out straight in front with elbows relaxed, holding the grips of the machine with the palms facing each other. Keeping the shoulder blades low, pull the grip toward the ribs. Return the arms to the original position slowly. Some *frequent problems* are tilting back when pulling the weight, curving the back, not bending the knees, or letting the weight yank the arms back to the original position.

LAT PULL-OVER — MUSCLES USED; MOVEMENTS PERFORMED; PROPER BODY POSITION:

The latissimus dorsi, teres major, and pectoralis major move the arms down in front of the body. The pectoralis minor and trapezius IV hold the shoulder blades down. The pectoralis minor and rhomboids spin the shoulder blades down. The pectoralis minor works to tip the shoulder blades up. The person lies on her back on a bench or the floor. The legs are bent, either on the floor or on the bench. Hold either a dumbbell or a barbell at chest level, arms close to the body, and hands over the bar with palms facing out or both wrapped around the weight on one side of the dumbbell. The torso should be very tight and the back either pressed to the floor or bench or in a relaxed position. Lift the weight up and over the head and return to the chest.

LAT PULL-OVER — FREQUENT PROBLEMS; TRAINER'S RESPONSIBILITY FOR SPOTTING; WAYS TO CHANGE ACTIVITY FOR INDIVIDUAL LEVEL OF FITNESS:

Frequent problems include letting the back sway while lifting the weight. The person may try to drop the elbows out to the sides, but they should be kept straight and close to the body and head as the weight is lifted. The trainer must remain near the person's head and hold his hands under the weight for the entire activity. This activity should not be attempted by anyone who is not fit. More fit people can increase the workload by lying on an exercise ball. In addition, a more fit person could sit on an exercise ball and catch a medicine ball instead of lifting a weight, leaning back into a lat pull-over, then sitting back up and throwing the ball to another person.

TRICEPS KICKBACK (or TRICEPS EXTENSION)—MUSCLES USED; MOVEMENTS PERFORMED; PROPER BODY POSITION:

The triceps work to straighten the elbow. The person places one knee and the hand of the same side on a bench. The back is straight and parallel to the floor. The opposite foot is flat on the floor, while the opposite arm (working arm) is bent at a right angle with the dumbbell hanging down and palm facing in. The upper arm should be raised and parallel to the back, but close to the body. The torso is tight. Slowly straighten the arm so that the weight moves back toward the buttocks, and is raised to the height of the back. The elbow remains close to the body. Slowly lower the weight to return to the original bent arm position.

TRICEPS KICKBACK—FREQUENT PROBLEMS; TRAINER'S RESPONSIBILITY; WAYS TO CHANGE ACTIVITY FOR INDIVIDUAL LEVEL OF FITNESS:

Some ***frequent problems*** that occur with this activity include throwing the arm backward as it is straightened rather than deliberately controlling the motion. Other problems include not keeping the back straight, shrugging the shoulders or lowering the upper arm. ***The trainer*** should stay near the side, either holding his hand under the weight, or placing a hand on the back to help balance the torso. For less fit people, standing triceps press-downs or supine elbow extensions may be substituted. More fit people may want to work both arms simultaneously, or stand upright and perform the activity on one leg. Instead of kneeling on a bench, a more fit person could lie face down on an exercise ball to perform the triceps kickback.

STANDING TRICEPS PRESS-DOWN — MUSCLES USED; MOVEMENTS PERFORMED; PROPER BODY POSITION; FREQUENT PROBLEMS; TRAINER'S RESPONSIBILITY; WAYS TO CHANGE ACTIVITY FOR INDIVIDUAL LEVEL OF FITNESS:

The triceps are used to straighten the elbow. Using a high-pulley cable column, stand facing the machine with feet apart, knees slightly bent, and torso tight. Grab the bar with palms facing outward, and pull down to the shoulder. Keeping the shoulder blades low and the upper arms close to the side and still, pull the bar down to thighs using only the forearms and elbow. Release the weight slowly. Wrists should stay in a straight position.

Frequent problems include letting the weight yank the arms, tilting the whole body forward and back when pulling and releasing the weight, or letting the wrists, shoulders or shoulder blades move. ***The trainer*** should hold her arms close to the person's upper arms to remind him to keep the shoulders from moving. Less fit people should use lighter weights. More fit people can do the activity while standing on only one leg.

SEATED TRICEPS EXTENSION—MUSCLES USED; MOVEMENTS PERFORMED; PROPER BODY POSITION; FREQUENT PROBLEMS; TRAINER'S RESPONSIBILITY; WAYS TO CHANGE ACTIVITY FOR INDIVIDUAL LEVEL OF FITNESS:

The triceps straighten the elbows. If sitting, feet should be on the floor. If standing, feet should be apart and balanced, with knees slightly bent. Torso should be tight. Arms are over the head,

- 83 -

elbows straight with dumbbell in both hands over the head. Keeping elbows close to the head, bend the arms so the dumbbell is lowered behind the head. Upper arms should stay still. **Frequent problems** include letting the elbows move away from the head, bending the back or not keeping the upper arms and shoulders still. **The trainer** should hold his hands near the weight as it is lifted and lowered. Less flexible people should avoid this they cannot get the shoulders into the position. More fit people can try this activity with one arm at a time, or while sitting on an exercise ball with either both feet on the floor or with one foot raised.

SUPINE ELBOW EXTENSION—MUSCLES USED; MOVEMENTS PERFORMED; PROPER BODY POSITION:

The triceps work to straighten the arms. The person lies on her back on a bench or the floor, with knees bent up and feet near the buttocks. If the person is fit, she can place feet on the floor while lying on the bench, as long as the back is pressed to the bench. The torso should be tight. Hold the dumbbell in the air with both hands, arms straight but elbows relaxed. Moving only the forearms, lower the dumbbell just over the head. Elbows will point up. Slowly return the dumbbell to the up position. This can also be done with a barbell or two dumbbells. When using a barbell, the palms should face away from the body, and the bar should be lowered to the forehead. If using two dumbbells, they should be lowered to the sides of the head near the ears, with palms facing in.

SUPINE ELBOW EXTENSION—FREQUENT PROBLEMS; TRAINER'S RESPONSIBILITY; WAYS TO CHANGE ACTIVITY FOR INDIVIDUAL LEVEL OF FITNESS:

Frequent problems include dropping the weight and injuring the head. Overextending the elbows or letting them fall out to the sides are also frequent problems. Many people will also tip the upper arms or arch the back during the activity. **The trainer** should hold her hands near the weight in order to catch it if it falls toward the person's head. Less fit people can raise the legs up higher for more back support if necessary. More fit people can use two dumbbells, or work one arm at a time. If working one arm at a time, the opposite arm should hold the upper arm for more stability. More fit people can also do the activity on an exercise ball, or on a ball or roller with a leg lifted.

TRICEPS DIP—MUSCLES USED; MOVEMENTS PERFORMED; PROPER BODY POSITION; FREQUENT PROBLEMS:

The triceps straighten the elbow. The anterior deltoid and pectoralis major bend the arms at the shoulder (shoulder flexion). The person should stand with his back toward a bench or a dip machine, placing hands on the edge of the bench (if using) or on the bars. Arms are straight. The torso is tight. The weight of the body is held by the arms, so if using a bench, the knees should be bent so as not to support the body's weight and pelvis is close to the bench. Bend the elbows so that the body is let down slowly until the upper arms are horizontal, then straighten the elbows to raise the body up. The shoulder blades and shoulders should stay low throughout the activity. **Frequent problems** include dropping too far down and putting too much stress on the shoulders or letting the elbows drop out to the sides.

ALTERNATE DUMBBELL BICEPS CURL—MUSCLES USED; MOVEMENTS PERFORMED; PROPER BODY POSITION; FREQUENT PROBLEMS:

The biceps, brachialis and brachioradialis bend the elbows. The supinator turns the forearm so that the palm faces up. The person should sit or stand, feet apart and balanced, with torso tight. If standing, the knees should be bent a little. Shoulder blades and shoulders should stay low and still. Hold dumbbell in each hand down near the thigh, palms facing in. Lift one forearm and turn the arm so that the palm faces up. Keep the upper arm still and the wrists in a straight

- 84 -

position. Lower and turn the arm again to return to the original position. Do the activity with the other arm, and take turns with each arm for the desired number of times. **Frequent problems** include swaying the arms or the torso, shrugging the shoulders, and moving the wrists or upper arms.

CONCENTRATION CURL—MUSCLES USED; MOVEMENTS PERFORMED; PROPER BODY POSITION; FREQUENT PROBLEMS:
The biceps, brachialis and brachioradialis are used to bend the elbows. The person should sit on a bench with knees bent and legs far apart. The arm with the dumbbell should rest on the inside of the thigh of the same side. The palm is facing up and holding the dumbbell with the elbow straight. The other hand rests on the knee. Lift the dumbbell up towards the head, keeping palm up, wrists stable and the upper arm still. The elbow should stay pressed against the thigh. Lower the weight to the original position without overextending the elbow. **Frequent problems** include letting the wrists fall out of a stable position, shrugging the shoulders, or letting the arm overextend at the elbow.

PREACHER BENCH CURLS—MUSCLES USED; MOVEMENTS PERFORMED; PROPER BODY POSITION; FREQUENT PROBLEMS; TRAINER'S RESPONSIBILITY FOR SPOTTING:
The biceps, brachialis and brachioradialis work to bend the elbows. The person should sit or stand facing the preacher bench or curl bar. Upper arms should lean on the bench pad, diagonally positioned out from the shoulders, elbows facing forward. If standing, feet should be slightly apart and balanced. The torso is tight and the back is straight. The chest should be against the pad. Hold the barbell or dumbbells with palms facing up. Beginning with the arms straight, bend the arm and raise the dumbbells as far up toward the shoulders as possible, keeping the upper arms and wrists still. Lower the weight again, keeping the elbow from overextending. **Frequent problems** include moving the upper arms or wrists, curving the back or shrugging the shoulders, or overextending the elbows. **The trainer** should hold her hand near the weight to keep it from dropping and overextending the elbow.

STANDING BARBELL CURLS—MUSCLES USED; MOVEMENTS PERFORMED; PROPER BODY POSITION; FREQUENT PROBLEMS; VARIATIONS OF THIS CURL:
The biceps, brachialis and brachioradialis bend the elbow. The person stands with feet apart and balanced, torso tight, and shoulders and shoulder blades low. Holding the barbell in front of the thighs with palms facing up, keeping upper arms still, raise the bar to the shoulders. Lower the bar without letting the weight yank the arms. **Frequent problems** include swinging the torso and upper arms to get momentum to help lift the weight. The elbows may overextend on the return motion, or the shoulders shrug when lifting the weight. This can be done seated or with the back against a wall. This activity can also be done with the palms facing down on the barbell in order to focus on the brachialis. It is then called the reverse curl. If the person sits and uses dumbbells (palms facing in), it is called the hammer curl.

PALMS-UP (SUPINATED) WRIST CURL and PALMS-DOWN (PRONATED) WRIST CURL—MUSCLES USED; MOVEMENTS PERFORMED; PROPER BODY POSITION; FREQUENT PROBLEMS:
The flexor carpi radialis and flexor carpi ulnaris bend the wrists in the palms-up wrist curl. The extensor carpi radialis longus, extensor carpi radialis brevis, and extensor carpi ulnaris straighten the wrists in the palms-down wrist curl. For the palms-up curl, the person sits and places arms on a pad or on the thighs, with palms facing up, one dumbbell in each hand. The back should be straight, torso tight, and feet firmly planted and balanced. The shoulder blades and shoulders should stay low. Lift and lower the weights slowly with only the wrists, keeping the forearms on the pad or thighs and the hands relaxed. For the palms-down curl, the position is

the same except the palms are facing down, so the lifting of weights is done in reverse from the palms-up version. *Frequent problems* include holding the dumbbells too hard, shrugging the shoulders or curving the back.

PELVIC TILT and HOLLOWING FOR ABDOMINALS—PROPER BODY POSITION:

The person should lie on her back on the floor with the knees bent and feet on the floor. The back should be relaxed, arms at the sides (near the hips), and buttocks, legs and feet relaxed. For the motion, press the back into the floor keeping the rest of the body relaxed. The muscles of the abdomen should move in toward the back. Then relax the torso and allow the back to return to a comfortable position. The person should breathe in during the relaxed position and breathe out as the muscles are drawn in. This is particularly important to this activity. This motion is very subtle and is designed to provide the person with the ability to pay closer attention to the body and give some stability for the torso muscles.

PELVIC TILT and HOLLOWING FOR ABDOMINALS—MUSCLES USED; MOVEMENTS PERFORMED; FREQUENT PROBLEMS; TRAINER'S RESPONSIBILITY FOR SPOTTING; WAYS TO CHANGE ACTIVITY FOR INDIVIDUAL LEVEL OF FITNESS:

The rectus abdominus is used to bend the lower back and tip the pelvis back. The transverse abdominis is used to force breath out and press the torso muscles in. Some *frequent problems* include arching the back when returning to the original position, or incorrect breathing technique. Some people will also try to move the hips instead of using only the torso to perform the motion. *The trainer* should hold the hand over the abdomen (with the person's permission) to remind her to hold the torso muscles down. This is a good exercise for even less fit people. More fit people can do this activity while tilted on a board, or on an exercise ball.

HIP LIFT—MUSCLES USED; MOVEMENTS PERFORMED; PROPER BODY POSITION; FREQUENT PROBLEMS; TRAINER'S RESPONSIBILITY FOR SPOTTING; WAYS TO CHANGE ACTIVITY FOR INDIVIDUAL LEVEL OF FITNESS:

The rectus abdominis, internal obliques and external obliques bend the lower back. The rectus abdominis also tips the pelvis back. The transverse abdominis forces breath out and presses the torso muscles in. The person should lie on his back, with both legs raised in the air at a right angle to the body. The arms can be laid over the chest, resting near the hips, or holding the back of the head. Pull the hips up and in toward chest while leaving the angle of the hips and legs the same. Some *frequent problems* include swaying the legs and hips, pushing down with the arms to gain lift, or not breathing. *The trainer* should hold her hands over the stomach to remind the person to hold the torso in. Less fit people should do abdominal curls instead. More fit people can lie on a tilted bench with the head up.

ABDOMINAL CURL—MUSCLES USED; MOVEMENTS PERFORMED; PROPER BODY POSITION; FREQUENT PROBLEMS; WAYS TO CHANGE ACTIVITY FOR INDIVIDUAL LEVEL OF FITNESS:

The rectus abdominis, internal obliques and external obliques bend the back. The transverse abdominis forces breath out and presses the torso in. The person should lie on his back. Legs are bent, with feet on the floor. Arms may be behind head, lying over the chest or anywhere the person finds comfortable. Tighten the torso muscles, pulling in toward the back. Curl the upper body and back toward the hips so that the shoulders are raised. *Frequent problems* include tugging the neck out of a straight position or letting the torso muscle relax (thus the tummy poking out instead of pulling in) when lifting.

Less fit people can do this activity with the legs up against a wall or on a tilted bench (head up). More fit people can do this activity on a slanted bench (head down), on an exercise ball, or with one leg in the air.

SUPINE CRUNCH TWIST—MUSCLES USED; MOVEMENTS PERFORMED; PROPER BODY POSITION; FREQUENT PROBLEMS; WAYS TO CHANGE ACTIVITY FOR INDIVIDUAL LEVEL OF FITNESS:

The internal obliques and external obliques bend the back while twisting it. The transverse abdominis forces breath out and presses the torso in. The person should lie on her back. The legs can be bent, one leg may be crossed over the opposite thigh or the legs can be straight out with one ankle over the other. One or both arms can be behind the head or straight out in front. Tighten the torso and raise the shoulders, twisting the chest simultaneously. One shoulder may remain on the floor. Return to original position slowly.

Frequent problems include pulling the neck out of a straight position, or tilting the shoulder and elbow instead of lifting the upper body. Less fit people can place the feet on a bench. More fit people can do this activity on a tipped board (head down), on an exercise ball, or while raising one leg.

ABDOMINAL EXERCISE MACHINE—STEPS TO TAKE TO HELP MAKE SURE CLIENT IS ISOLATING THE TORSO AND BACK MUSCLES INSTEAD OF HIPS:

The trainer should adjust the height of the machine so that the part of the machine that will rotate to move the person into a bending position is located along the lowest part of the chest rather than near the hips. Have the person focus on pulling the chest and the hips in together. When using a standing roman chair (similar to a triceps dip bar), the person should have a lot of strength before attempting. The person should hold the weight of the body up with the upper arms, then lift the bent legs until the thighs are parallel to the floor. The trainer should make sure the angle of the hips at that point is held for the second part of the activity. Then, the torso muscles should be used to curl the hips up (keeping the same hip angle) very slowly rather than swinging the legs.

SEATED BACK EXTENSION MACHINE—MUSCLES USED; MOVEMENTS PERFORMED; PROPER BODY POSITION; FREQUENT PROBLEMS:

The erector spinae work to straighten the back. The gluteus maximus and the hamstrings work to straighten the hips. The person should sit on the seated back extension machine, feet on the pads and hands on the handles. The lap belt should be buckled to keep the thighs from moving. The seat should be adjusted so that the point that will be going around will be near the lower back. If the hips are to be worked, the point that will be going around can go closer to the hips. The person then pushes the weight backwards, lying back and straightening the hips. Some ***problems*** that can happen include the person swinging his upper body to move the machine instead of isolating the muscles to move the machine. In addition, using too much weight can cause injury, so it should be avoided.

PRONE BACK EXTENSION (COBRA)—MUSCLES USED; MOVEMENTS PERFORMED; PROPER BODY POSITION; WAYS TO CHANGE ACTIVITY FOR INDIVIDUAL LEVEL OF FITNESS:

The erector spinae work to straighten the back and curl it backwards. The person should lie face down on the floor, torso and buttocks muscles tight. The arms are at the sides. The neck is straight and relaxed and the chin pointing toward the floor. The shoulder blades are low and relaxed. The shoulders and head are lifted off the floor slowly and held for a short pause, then lowered. Less fit people can place their hands down on the floor just in front of their face, elbows bent and raise themselves up with the support of the arms. More fit people can do this activity with one arm out in front on the floor with the other at the side. In addition, more fit people can do this activity on an exercise ball or with a twist in the back.

BACK EXTENSION ON A ROMAN CHAIR—MUSCLES USED; MOVEMENTS PERFORMED; PROPER BODY POSITION; FREQUENT PROBLEMS; WAYS TO CHANGE ACTIVITY FOR INDIVIDUAL LEVEL OF FITNESS:

The erector spinae are used to straighten the lower back. The gluteus maximus and the hamstrings are used to straighten the hips. The person should lie face down with the waist on the pad. The knees are placed under the knee bar for stability. The arms can be in any comfortable position. The closer the arms are to the torso, the easier the activity will be. Begin by bending at the waist, then lift the upper torso slowly. Slowly lower the upper body down. Possible **problems** include the person moving too quickly and swinging the torso up and down instead of slowly isolating the movement. In addition, only extremely fit people should attempt to lift the torso higher than the hips. Bending the back in this way might cause injury in someone with less trained muscles. This activity should not be attempted by less fit people.

SUPINE HEEL SLIDES—MUSCLES USED; MOVEMENTS PERFORMED; PROPER BODY POSITION:

The supine heel slide is designed to practice keeping the torso still and the torso muscles tight while doing other activities with different parts of the body. Back and abdominal muscles worked are the rectus abdominus, the external obliques, the internal obliques, the transverse abdominis, the quadratus lumborum, the erector spinae, and the mulifidus.
The shoulder blade muscles worked are the trapezius, the rhomboids, the pectoralis minor, the serratus anterior and the levator scapulae. These muscles will remain still while the legs or arms move. The person lies on her back, with the torso muscles tight and the back in a normal position. Although the abdomen is tight, the back is not pressed into the floor. The knees are bent and arms at the sides near the hips. One foot slides out, straightening that knee. Pull the foot back in, bending the knee again. Alternate with the opposite leg.

SUPINE HEEL SLIDES—FREQUENT PROBLEMS; TRAINER'S RESPONSIBILITY FOR SPOTTING; WAYS TO CHANGE ACTIVITY FOR INDIVIDUAL LEVEL OF FITNESS:

Frequent problems encountered during supine heel slides include letting the back curve up instead of staying in a normal position, lifting the shoulder blades, or letting the torso muscles relax or protrude during the activity.
The trainer may hold his hands over the torso to remind the person to hold her muscles in. He might also hold his hands under the person's back in order to remind her not to press the back in. This motion is very subtle and people new to exercise may need help noticing the subtle differences between good placement and poor placement. This exercise is a good beginner activity for less fit people. More fit people can perform the dead bug exercise, lifting the knee toward the chest and lifting the arm on the same side instead of sliding the heels.

QUADRUPED ACTIVITY—MUSCLES USED; MOVEMENTS PERFORMED; PROPER BODY POSITION:

Similar to the supine heel slide, the quadruped activity is designed to practice keeping the torso still and the torso muscles tight while doing other activities with different parts of the body. Back and abdominal muscles worked are the rectus abdominus, the external obliques, the internal obliques, the transverse abdominis, the quadratus lumborum, the erector spinae, and the mulifidus. The shoulder blade muscles worked are the trapezius, the rhomboids, the pectoralis minor, the serratus anterior and the levator scapulae. These muscles will remain still while the legs or arms move. The person gets onto hands and knees facing the floor, with the torso muscles pulled up, and the back and neck straight. Lift one leg so that it is even with the hips and back, then lift the opposite arm to the same height, and hold the position for a little while. Alternate with the opposite leg and arm.

- 88 -

PLANK—MUSCLES USED; MOVEMENTS PERFORMED; PROPER BODY POSITION:

This activity is designed to keep the abdominal muscles stable. Back and abdominal muscles worked are the rectus abdominus, the external obliques, the internal obliques, the transverse abdominis, the quadratus lumborum, the erector spinae, and the mulifidus. The shoulder blade muscles worked are the trapezius, the rhomboids, the pectoralis minor, the serratus anterior and the levator scapulae. The person positions himself on the floor, facing down, with weight on hands and toes. The back is straight and the abdomen tight, the hands are positioned just below shoulders, and the elbows bent a little bit. The shoulder blades are relaxed. The position is held for a little while and then released. No actual motion is performed.

PLANK—FREQUENT PROBLEMS; TRAINER'S RESPONSIBILITY FOR SPOTTING; WAYS TO CHANGE ACTIVITY FOR INDIVIDUAL LEVEL OF FITNESS:

Problems that can occur are letting the torso sag and the back sway, shrugging the shoulders or pulling the shoulder blades back, not keeping the elbows bent, or straining the neck. The trainer should hold his hand under the torso to remind the person to keep the muscles tight. Less fit people can do this activity on knees instead of toes or on the forearms instead of the hands. More fit people can do this activity while lifting one leg, while bending elbows in a "push-up" position, or by doing a plank with only one side of the body, and the opposing arm in the air and the opposing leg resting on top of the working leg, or held up in the air.

KNEE EXTENSIONS—MUSCLES USED; MOVEMENTS PERFORMED; PROPER BODY POSITION; FREQUENT PROBLEMS:

The quadriceps, rectus femoris, vastus lateralis, vastus intermedius, vastus medialis work to straighten the knee. The person sits on a knee extension machined. The point where the machine will go around should be adjusted to be close to the knees. Hold the handles with the palms facing in. The torso muscles are tight, and the back in a normal position. Knees are bent and the feet tucked under the pad. Straighten the leg slowly, lifting the pad with the weights. At the peak of the lift, a pause can be added to tighten the thigh muscles even more to increase the workload. Return slowly to the original position. **Problems** that can occur include using too much weight, swinging the legs instead of using slow and controlled movement, and moving the hips or back.

KNEE FLEXION MACHINE—MUSCLES USED; MOVEMENTS PERFORMED; PROPER BODY POSITION; FREQUENT PROBLEMS:

The hamstrings (biceps femoris, semitendinosus and semimembranosus) are used to bend the knee. The person sits on the machine (or may lie face down or stand on some machines). The hips must be stabilized by the thigh pad so they do not move. The back and head should lean against the back pad. The torso must be kept in a normal position and still. The backs of the ankles should be against the weighted pad, and as the knees bend, the ankles push against the pad to lift the weights. Straighten the legs slowly to return to the original position. **Some problems** that may occur include letting the ankle bar push the knees past the straight position into an overextended position. The hips or back may also move, or the person may swing the legs instead of using a controlled motion.

LEG PRESS MACHINE EXERCISE—MUSCLES USED; MOVEMENTS PERFORMED; PROPER BODY POSITION; FREQUENT PROBLEMS; WAYS TO CHANGE ACTIVITY FOR INDIVIDUAL LEVEL OF FITNESS:

The gluteus maximus and hamstrings straighten the hips, the quadriceps straighten the knees, and the gastrocnemius and the soleus point and flex the foot. The person sits on the leg press machine, leaning back into the pad, with the feet on the foot rest. The knees should be bent at a right angle. The torso muscles are tight. Press the feet and legs so that the knees and hips are straightened. The body will slide back on the machine. Slowly bend the knees to return to the original position. Some **problems** that could occur are moving too quickly into the knees-straight position, and overextending the knees or bending or arching the back. Less fit people can begin the activity with the knees bent less. More fit people can do the activity one leg at a time, or add a foot flex at the peak of the lift.

SQUATS—MUSCLES USED; MOVEMENTS PERFORMED; PROPER BODY POSITION:
The gluteus maximus and hamstrings straighten the hips. The quadriceps straighten the knees. The gastrocnemius and the soleus point and flex the feet. The person begins by standing with feet wide and flat on the floor. If using a weight, the hands can hold a barbell with palms facing down. The barbell should begin resting on the backs of the shoulders. The torso muscles are tight and the back is straight. Bend at the knees and hips so that the buttocks move backward. The knees should stay behind the tips of the toes. When the thighs are almost horizontal, lift the body and the weight up to return to the original position.

SQUATS—FREQUENT PROBLEMS; TRAINER'S RESPONSIBILITY FOR SPOTTING; WAYS TO CHANGE ACTIVITY FOR INDIVIDUAL LEVEL OF FITNESS:
Some **problems** that could occur include letting the hips get lower than the knees, or letting the knees move forward in front of the toes. With very heavy weights, the back may have a hard time getting back into the original position. Sometimes the person's feet will try to raise up on the toes. **The trainer** should stand behind the person and remind them to keep their back straight, knees back, and hips bent. If the person is using a weight, the trainer should hold her hands near the weight. Less fit people should do the sit-back squat (holding a stable support while sitting down) or a wall squat while using an exercise ball against the wall for support. More fit people can do the activity in combination with another activity such as a leg lift or a jump, or do the activity on one leg at a time.

LUNGES—MUSCLES USED; MOVEMENTS PERFORMED; PROPER BODY POSITION; FREQUENT PROBLEMS; TRAINER'S RESPONSIBILITY FOR SPOTTING:
The gluteus maximus and the hamstrings straighten the hips. The quadriceps straighten the knees. The gastrocnemius and the soleus point and flex the ankle. The person stands with legs apart. Hold dumbbells (if using) at the sides, palms facing in. The back is straight and the torso muscles are tight. The shoulders and shoulder blades are relaxed. Keeping the back straight, step one leg forward, rolling the foot from heel to toe and bending the knee until the thigh is horizontal. The knee stays behind the toes. The back leg is either straight or bent, but the back heel should be up. Pull the front foot back to the original position, keeping balance. Some **problems** that can occur include losing balance, not stepping far enough, bending the back, or not keeping the knees behind the toes. **The trainer** will not be able to easily spot this activity.

HIP ABDUCTION AND ADDUCTION MACHINE—MUSCLES USED; MOVEMENTS PERFORMED; PROPER BODY POSITION; FREQUENT PROBLEMS:
The gluteus medius works to swing the raised thigh out to the side. The adductor longus, adductor magnus, adductor brevis, gracilias and the pectineus are used to swing the raised thigh in towards the opposite leg. The person sits on the machine with back against the pad. The outsides of the knees are pressed against the leg pads while the hips are perpendicular to the torso. The torso is tight and the hands are holding the handles for stability. Press the knees and thighs outward. Slowly release the weights until just before the original position. The alternate position is to adjust the knee pads so that they are on the inside of the knees, and then press the legs in toward each other. Some **problems** include dropping the weights on the return, shrugging the shoulders, or stopping the press before reaching the peak of the activity.

SIDE-LYING HIP ABDUCTION AND ADDUCTION—PROPER BODY POSITION:

For the **adduction**, the person lies on the floor on one side, arm under the head, with the neck and arm making a line with the back. The hips are on top of each other and perpendicular to the floor. The legs are straight out or bent at the hip slightly. Knees can be bent or straight. The top arm is lightly held on the floor in front of the abdomen for support. The top leg is bent at the hip and held out in front, and can be rested on a bench. The lower leg is lifted as the torso is tightened, then lowered. Only the bottom leg should move while the rest of the body remains still. For the **abduction**, the body is in the same position as the adduction, but the bottom leg is bent slightly at the knee while the top leg is lifted up.

SIDE-LYING HIP ABDUCTION AND ADDUCTION—MUSCLES USED; MOVEMENTS PERFORMED; FREQUENT PROBLEMS; TRAINER'S RESPONSIBILITY FOR SPOTTING; WAYS TO CHANGE ACTIVITY FOR INDIVIDUAL LEVEL OF FITNESS:

The gluteus maximus works to swing the thigh out to the side. The adductor longus, adductor magnus, adductor brevis, gracilis, and pectinus work to swing the thigh in toward the other leg. Some **problems** that can occur include letting the hips sway to the front or back, or resting the head in the hand so that the neck is tilted. **The trainer** should make sure the hips do not sway and the torso is straight and tight. Less fit people should do this activity without weights. More fit people may do this activity with ankle weights, or by lifting both legs while holding an exercise ball between them.

HEEL RAISES—MUSCLES USED; MOVEMENTS PERFORMED; PROPER BODY POSITION; FREQUENT PROBLEMS; WAYS TO CHANGE ACTIVITY FOR INDIVIDUAL LEVEL OF FITNESS:

The gastrocnemius and the soleus work to flex and point the ankle. The person stands on a step or low bench with heels hanging off the side. Legs are apart, torso is tight, and the back is straight. If dumbbells are being used, face the palms in. The shoulders and shoulder blades should be relaxed. The knees are not locked, but not bent. Lift the body with only the balls of the foot so that the heels, which begin by being lower than the step, are raised to a level above the step. Lower to the original position.

Some **problems** that can occur include moving too quickly and stretching the Achilles tendon, bending the knees instead of the ankles, or letting the back move out of a straight position. Less fit people can hold a support beam. More fit people can do the activity with one leg at a time.

DORSIFLEXION AND EVERSION—MUSCLES USED; MOVEMENTS PERFORMED; PROPER BODY POSITION; TRAINER'S RESPONSIBILITY FOR SPOTTING:

The anterior tibialis, extensor digitorum longus, and the peroneus tertius work to flex the ankle. The peroneus tertius, peroneus longus, peroneus brevis, and the extensor digitorum longus work to turn the foot outward. The person sits either with the back against a wall or with the hands at the sides, torso tight. **The trainer** puts an elastic band around the foot, and pulls the foot down from the top into a pointed position. The person pulls the foot back toward the leg resisting the elastic band. Then the trainer will adjust the band and pull the foot inward while the person turns the foot outward, resisting the band. The trainer must hold the elastic band for this activity.

LEVER REVIEW

There are three classes (kinds) of levers. A class-1 lever has its fulcrum located somewhere between the effort and the load. The direction of force is changed with this type of lever. Applying effort downward moves the load up and applying effort upward moves the load down. Examples of class-1 levers that you may be familiar with are the playground seesaw, a crowbar, scissors, and pliers.

First Class Lever

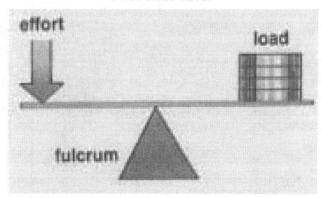

With a class-2 lever, the fulcrum is at one end, the effort is at the other end and the load is in the middle. With this kind of lever, the direction of effort is not changed. Pushing up on the lever arm pushes up on the load. A wheelbarrow is a class-2 lever. Effort is applied to the handles of the wheelbarrow and the wheel is the fulcrum. The load sits close to the fulcrum.

Second Class Lever

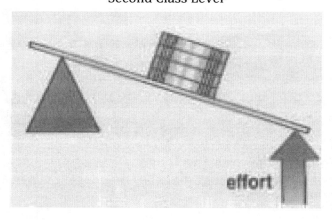

Another arrangement of the lever can be found in a class-3 lever. The fulcrum is at one end and the effort is applied between the fulcrum and the load. With this kind of lever, the direction of effort is not changed. The load moves in the same direction as the effort. You will find lots of class-3 levers being used in sporting activities! Baseball bats, hockey sticks, tennis rackets, and golf clubs all gain speed because the hitting end moves faster than your arm.

Third Class Lever

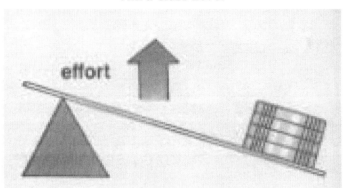

SARCOMERE REVIEW

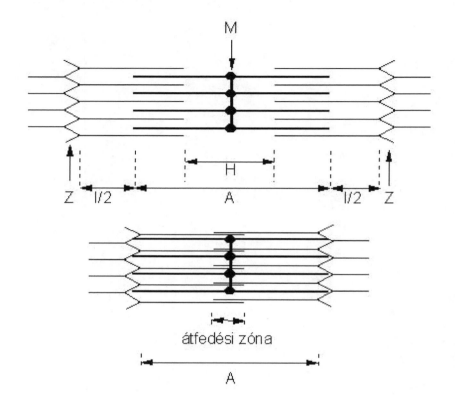

- Z-Disk: The union of two actin heads.

    - It demarcates the sarcomere.

    - At the Z-Disk, there is no myosin.

- A-Band: The distance of one thick filament, consisting of two myosin filaments.

- I-Band: The distance from the end of one thick filament to the beginning of the next thick filament.

    - During contraction, the I-Band becomes shorter.

    - The I-Band consists entirely of actin.

    - The I-Band marks the margins of two adjacent sarcomeres. Each I-Band technically lies within two sarcomeres.

- H-Zone: The distance from the end of one thin filament to the beginning of the next thin filament.

    - During contraction, the H-Zone becomes shorter.

    - The H-Zone consists entirely of myosin.

- The H-Zone lies completely within the sarcomere, near the center of the sarcomere.

In a myofibril, in cross section:

- Six actins can interact with each myosin. Actins are in a hexagonal array.

- Three Myosins can interact, in triangular fashion, with each actin.

Myosin plays the role of an ATPase Actin-Binding Motor Protein.

- When Myosin is bound to Actin, ATP is bound to the myosin head.

- With ATP bound, Myosin can then detach from the actin thin filament.

- Once detached, the myosin is free to hydrolyze the bound ATP to ADP + P_i. It hydrolyzes the ATP, and the ADP + P_i remain attached to the myosin head.

- The myosin then reattaches to the thin filament.

- Reattachment leads to the release of the Pi group, which in turn strengthens the interaction between the actin and myosin.

- Power Stroke: With the ATP gone, the myosin head undergoes a conformational change, causing the actin and myosin to move relative to each other.

- Then the myosin head releases the ADP.

- Then Another ATP must bind to the myosin, in order for the myosin to release from the Actin to start another cross-bridge.

    - If there is no more ATP, Rigor Mortis results, in which the muscle is stuck in the contractile state, with myosin bound to actin.

Relaxed State

- Tropomyosin is bound to the thin filament around its major groove, in the absence of calcium.

- The Troponin Complex is periodically bound to the thin filament such that it blocks the interaction between Actin and Myosin.

Contracted State

- Calcium binds to the Troponin Complex, causing a conformational change in Troponin-C.

- Troponin Complex (Troponin plus tropomyosin) removes itself from the thin filament as a result, such that Myosin can bind.

Neuromuscular Junction

- Active Zone: Electron-dense (dark in EM scan) patch of membrane at the end of a nerve, right at the neuromuscular junction.

  - Note that vesicles are found right at the membrane, while mitochondria are found more proximal, away from the active zone.

- Junctional Fold is right opposite the active zone.

- Ach Receptors on the muscle membrane are highly concentrated right at the nerve terminal.

Muscle Development:

- Mesenchymal cells form myoblasts.

- Myoblasts proliferate and form myotubes by fusing together, resulting in a large multinucleated cell.

- So, muscle becomes multinucleated by the fusing together of primitive myoblasts.

Satellite Cells: These cells lie squeezed in-between the endomysium (basement membrane) of a myofibril and the fibers themselves.

- Developmentally they have the same origin as myotubes. They are myoblasts that did not fuse with other myoblasts during development.

- They proliferate to repair damaged muscle tissue.

  - They will divide to regenerate muscle, but the regeneration may be incomplete.

Muscle Regeneration:

- When the muscle fibers are gone, all that is left is the basal lamina and reticular formation of the endomysium.

- The satellite cells then migrate into the empty endomysium.

- Macrophages come in to remove necrotic remnants (debris)

- Muscle regeneration may be incomplete (muscle atrophy or weakness).

- Fiber Splitting can occur, where the satellite cell can generate smaller duplicated myofibril sections from one original myofiber.

Penniform Muscle: Muscles with a central tendon, used for strength and stability. Ex)Transversus Abdominis.

Fusiform Muscle: Muscles with a tendon on either side longitudinally, used for speed. Ex) Biceps Brachii.

KEY MOVEMENT TERMS

Flexion is bending, most often ventrally to decrease the angle between two parts of the body; it is usually an action at an articulation or joint.

Extension is straightening, or increasing the angle between two parts of the body; a stretching out or making the flexed part straight.

Abduction is a movement away from the midsagittal plane (midline); to adduct is to move medially and bring a part back to the mid-axis.

Circumduction is a circular movement at a ball and socket (shoulder or hip) joint, utilizing the movements of flexion, extension, abduction, and adduction.

Rotation is a movement of a part of the body around its long axis.

Supination refers only to the movement of the radius around the ulna. In supination the palm of the hand is oriented anteriorly; turning the palm dorsally puts it into pronation. The body on its back is in the supine position.

Pronation refers to the palm of the hand being oriented posteriorly. The body on its belly is the prone position.

Inversion refers only to the lower extremity, specifically the ankle joint. When the foot (plantar surface) is turned inward, so that the sole is pointing and directed toward the midline of the body and is parallel with the median plane, we speak of inversion. Its opposite is eversion.

Eversion refers to the foot (plantar surface) being turned outward so that the sole is pointing laterally.

Opposition is one of the most critical movements in humans; it allows us to have pulp-to-pulp opposition, which gives us the great dexterity of our hands. In this movement the thumb pad is brought to a finger pad. A median nerve injury negates this action.

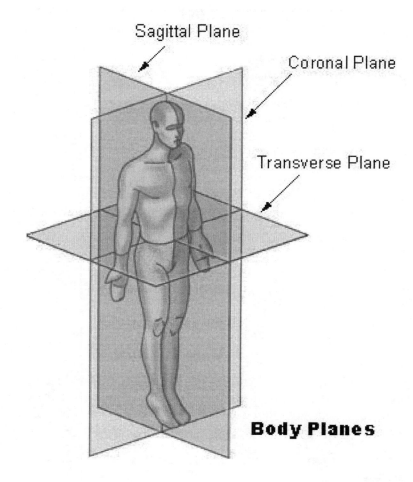

Sagittal Plane

Coronal Plane

Transverse Plane

Body Planes

GAIT CYCLE

The gait cycle can be described in the phasic terms of initial contact, loading response, midstance, terminal stance, preswing, initial swing, midswing and terminal swing. The stance period consists of the first five phases: initial contact, loading response, midstance, terminal stance and preswing. The swing period primarily is divided into three phases: initial swing, midswing and terminal swing. Preswing, however, prepares the limb for swing advancement and in that sense could be considered a component of swing phase.

Initial Contact
Initial contact is an instantaneous point in time only and occurs the instant the foot of the leading lower limb touches the ground. Most of the motor function that occurs during initial contact is in preparation for the loading response phase that will follow.
Initial contact represents the beginning of the stance phase. Heel strike and heel contact serve as poor descriptors of this period since there are many circumstances when initial contact is not made with the heel alone. The term "foot strike" sometimes is used as an alternative descriptor.

Loading Response

The loading response phase occupies about 10 percent of the gait cycle and constitutes the period of initial double-limb support. During loading response, the foot comes in full contact with the floor, and body weight is fully transferred onto the stance limb.

The initial double-support stance period occasionally is referred to as initial stance. The term foot flat is the point in time when the foot becomes plantar grade. The loading response period probably is best described by the typical quantified values of the vertical force curve. The ascending initial peak of the vertical force graph reveals the period of loading response.

Midstance

Midstance represents the first half of single support, which occurs from the 10- to 30-percent periods of the gait cycle. It begins when the contralateral foot leaves the ground and continues as the body weight travels along the length of the foot until it is aligned over the forefoot. The descending initial peak of the vertical force graph reveals the period of midstance.

Terminal Stance

Terminal stance constitutes the second half of single-limb support. It begins with heel rise and ends when the contralateral foot contacts the ground. Terminal stance occurs from the 30- to 50-percent periods of the gait cycle. During this phase, body weight moves ahead of the forefoot.

The term heel off is a descriptor useful in observational analysis and is the point during the stance phase when the heel leaves the ground. The ascending second peak of the vertical force graph demonstrates the period of terminal stance.

Roll off describes the period of late stance (from the 40- to 50- percent periods of the gait cycle) when there is an ankle plantarflexor moment and simultaneous power generation of the triceps surae to initiate advancement of the tibia over the fulcrum of the metatarsal heads in preparation for the next phase.

Preswing

Preswing is the terminal double-limb support period and occupies the last 12 percent of stance phase, from 50 percent to 62 percent. It begins when the contralateral foot contacts the ground and ends with ipsilateral toe off. During this period, the stance limb is unloaded and body weight is transferred onto the contralateral limb. The descending portion of the second peak of the vertical force graph demonstrates the period of preswing.

Terminal Contact

Terminal contact is a term rarely used, describes the instantaneous point in the gait cycle when the foot leaves the ground. It thus represents either the end of the stance phase or the beginning of swing phase. In pathologies where the foot never leaves the ground, the term foot drag is used. In foot drag, the termination of stance and the onset of swing may be somewhat arbitrary.

The termination of stance and the onset of swing is defined as the point where all portions of the foot have achieved motion relative to the floor. Likewise, the termination of swing and the onset of stance may be defined as the point when the foot ends motion relative to the floor. Toe off occurs when terminal contact is made with the toe.

Initial Swing

The initial one-third of the swing period, from the 62- to 75-percent periods of the gait cycle, is spent in initial swing. It begins the moment the foot leaves the ground and continues until maximum knee flexion occurs, when the swinging extremity is directly under the body and directly opposite the stance limb.

Midswing

Midswing occurs in the second third of the swing period, from the 75- to 85-percent periods of the gait cycle. Critical events include continued limb advancement and foot clearance. This phase begins following maximum knee flexion and ends when the tibia is in a vertical position.

Terminal Swing

In the final phase of terminal swing from the 85- to 100-percent periods of the gait cycle, the tibia passes beyond perpendicular, and the knee fully extends in preparation for heel contact.

Fluid Intake Recommendations

ACSM Guidelines On Fluid Intake For Exercise
It is recommended that individuals consume a nutritionally balanced diet and drink adequate fluids during the 24 hour period before an event, especially during the period that includes the meal prior to exercise, to promote proper hydration before exercise or competition.
It is recommended that individuals drink about 500 ml (about 17 fl oz) of fluid about 2 hours before exercise to promote adequate hydration and allow time for excretion of excess ingested water.
During exercise, athletes should start drinking early and at regular intervals in an attempt to consume fluids at a rate sufficient to replace all the water lost through sweating (i.e. body weight loss), or consume the maximal amount that can be tolerated.
It is recommended that ingested fluids be cooler than ambient temperature (between 15 and 22°C, 59 and 72°F) and flavoured to enhance palatability and promote fluid replacement. Fluid should be readily available and served in containers that allow adequate volumes to be ingested with ease and with minimal interruption of exercise.
Addition of proper amounts of carbohydrates and/or electrolytes to a fluid replacement solution is recommended for exercise events of duration greater than 1 h since it does not significantly impair water delivery to the body and may enhance performance. During exercise of less than 1 h, there is little evidence of physiological or physical performance differences between consuming a carbohydrate-electrolyte drink and plain water.
During intense exercise lasting longer than 1 hour, it is recommended that carbohydrates be ingested at a rate of 30-60 g/h to maintain oxidation of carbohydrate and delay fatigue. This rate of carbohydrate delivery can be achieved without compromising fluid delivery by drinking 600-1200 ml/h of solutions containing 4-8% carbohydrates (g/100 ml). The carbohydrates can be sugars (glucose or sucrose) or starch (e.g. maltodextrins).
Inclusion of sodium (0.5-0.7 g/1 of water) in the rehydration solution ingested during exercise lasting longer than 1 hour is recommended since it may be advantageous in enhancing

palatability, promoting fluid retention, and possibly preventing hyponatremia in certain individuals who drink excessive quantities of fluid. There is little physiological basis for the presence of sodium in an oral rehydration solution for enhancing intestinal water absorption as long as sodium is sufficiently available from the previous meal.

THE BASICS – Summary

Muscular strength
- Ability to generate force against some resistance
- Important to maintain normal levels of strength for normal healthy living
- Imbalance or weakness can impair normal function

Muscular endurance
- Ability to perform repetitive muscular contractions against some resistance
- Power
- Ability to generate force quickly
- Combination of strength and speed
- Performance is limited without power

Types of Skeletal Muscle Contraction

Isometric contraction
Contraction that produces muscle tension but no change in muscle length

Concentric contraction
Contraction that causes muscle shortening while tension increases to overcome some resistance

Eccentric Contraction
Resistance is greater than the muscular force being produced and muscle lengthens while producing tension

Factors That Determine Levels of Strength, Endurance and Power

- Size of Muscle
- Proportional to cross-sectional diameter of muscle fibers
- Increased cross-sectional area = increased strength and force production
- Hypertrophy - Increase in muscle size
- Atrophy - Decrease in muscle size
- Number of Muscle Fibers
- Strength is a function of the number and diameter of muscle fibers
- Number of fibers is inherited characteristic.

Neuromuscular Efficiency

Strength is directly related to efficiency of the neuromuscular system
Initial increases in strength during first 8-10 weeks are attributed to neuromuscular efficiency

Enhanced strength in 3 ways
- Increase motor unit recruitment
- Increase in firing rate
- Enhance synchronization of motor unit firing

Age
- Men and women increase strength throughout puberty and adolescence
- Peaks at age 20-25
- After age 25, max strength declines 1% annually
- Decline is related to physical activity
- Able to retard decline in performance through activity

Biomechanical Considerations
- Position of tendon attachment
- Length-Tension Relationship
- Length of muscle determines tension that can be created
- Varying lengths will produce varying tensions
- Determined by overlap of actin-myosin filaments

Overtraining
- Imbalance between exercise and recovery
- Training exceeds physiological and psychological capacity of individual
- Can have negative effect on strength training
- May result in psychological or physiological breakdown
- Injury, illness, and fatigue can be indicators

Physiology of Strength Development

Muscle Hypertrophy
- Hyperplasia – increase in number of muscle fibers
- Genetically determined and does not seem to increase with training
- Increased number of capillaries
- No new capillaries
- Increase in dormant capillary activity to meet needs of muscle
- Increased size and number of myofilaments
- Actin and myosin- Reversibility – adaptations of muscle due to training can begin to reverse within 48 hours of removing training

Techniques of Resistance Training

Overload Principle
- To improve strength, muscle must be worked at a level higher than it is accustomed to

- Muscle will maintain strength if it is trained against a consistent resistance that it is accustomed to
- Existence of current strength and will result in increased muscle endurance
- Effective training requires a consistently increasing effort against progressively more resistant loads
- Be mindful of pain when dealing with progression

Isometric Exercise
- Capable of increasing muscle strength at specific joint angles
- No corresponding increase at other joint angles
- May produce spikes in systolic blood pressure
- Could cause life-threatening cardiovascular accident
- To reduce likelihood of such an event, athlete should breath
- Attempt to use positional or functional exercise – work at multiple angles throughout the range if possible

Progressive Resistive Exercise
- Most popular and commonly used
- Exercises that work through a full range of motion
- Isotonic or isodynamic contractions
- Concentric vs. Eccentric
- Greater force can be generated due to lower number of motor units recruited allowing other motor units to be recruited to generate increased force
- Oxygen use is much lower with eccentrics
- Efficiency of eccentric exercise is higher than concentric exercise
- Needs of the body – acceleration and deceleration
- Must be able to control body movements – deceleration and eccentrics allows for this control

Free Weights vs. Exercise Machines
- Machines - Safety and easy to use, constraints on motion and generally single plane of motion
- Free weights – do not restrict motion and incorporate certain level of neuromuscular control
- Variable Resistance
- Change in force required at different angles to move a particular resistance
- Greatest when joint is at 90 degrees
- Accommodating resistance or variable resistance equipment changes resistance at different points in range

Recommended Techniques of Resistance Training

Must consider 4 areas
- Amount of weight to be used
- Number of repetitions
- Number of sets
- Frequency of training

Multiple potential routines
- Single set – 1 set 8-12 reps at a slow speed
- Tri-sets – 3 exercises for 1 muscle group, 2-4 sets with no rest
- Multiple sets – 2-3 warm-up sets with progressively increasing resistance followed by several sets at the same resistance
- Superset – multiple exercises, 1 set of 8-10 repetitions or 1 or 2 exercises, with multiple sets of 8-10 repetitions
- Pyramid – multiple sets decreasing repetitions and increasing resistance
- Split routine – Workouts exercise different groups of muscles on different days

Isokinetic Exercise
- Involves muscle contractions where length change of muscle is set at a constant velocity
- Maximal resistance throughout the range of motion
- Variety of machines/manufacturers are available
- Can be used with eccentrics and concentric exercise

Isokinetics as a Conditioning Tool
- Maximal effort for maximal strength gains
- Dynamometer will move at a set speed whether maximal or half of maximal effort is put forth
- Athlete can cheat with machine and not put forth the effort
- Not cost effective
- Training at fast vs. slow speeds
- Functional speeds

Open vs. Closed Kinetic Chain Exercises
- Anatomical and functional relationships that exist in the upper and lower extremity
- Open kinetic chain- Foot or hand not in contact with ground or some other surface
- Closed kinetic chain- Foot or hand is weight bearing
- Most activities call for weight bearing of foot or hand in some capacity
- May be more functional than open chain activities in some instances

Training for Muscular Strength vs. Muscular Endurance

Strength and endurance are closely related
- As one improves, the tendency is for the other to do the same
- For strength development- Heavier weight and low repetitions should be used
- Endurance training- Lighter weight and high repetitions (10-15) are suggested

Additional Terminology

- Partials: Doing a movement through a small range of motion. Usually used to strengthen the weak part of a lift. Also commonly seen when the person is using too much weight and can't do the full movement.

- Negatives: Using a weight that's above your max and only perform the negative portion (The part of the activity where the weight is moving with gravity). Spotters lift the weight through the positive area and you do the negatives.

- Stripping: Doing a set to failure then the spotters remove some weight and you do a few more reps to failure.

- Burns: After positive failure occurs, continue doing mini-reps (a few inches of movement) to keep stress on the muscles.

- 21's: Do half of the movement for 7 reps, then do the other half for 7 reps then do 7 full reps. i.e. Barbell curl: Curl from arms straight to 90 degrees for 7 reps. Then curl from 90 degrees to arms perpendicular to floor for 7 reps. Then do 7 full reps.

ENDURANCE

Endurance exercises are any activities that increase the heart rate and breathing for an extended period of time. Listed below are daily activities that your client may perform to help build endurance. They vary from moderate to vigorous. Moderate activities won't "break" a sweat as quickly as vigorous.

Moderate Activities
    Bicycling
    Cycling on a stationary bicycle
    Dancing
    Gardening (mowing, raking)
    Mopping or scrubbing floor
    Golf, without a cart
    Rowing
    Swimming
    Tennis (doubles)
    Volleyball
    Walking briskly on a level surface

Vigorous Activities
    Brisk bicycling up hills
    Climbing stairs or hills
    Cross-country skiing
    Digging holes
    Downhill skiing
    Hiking
    Jogging
    Shoveling snow
    Swimming laps
    Tennis (singles)

Bicycling

Another good endurance activity is bicycling. Exercising on an indoor, stationary bicycle is a good way to improve a client's endurance without putting too much stress on their hips, knees, and feet.

Cycling Tips
- Keep your knees almost straight when the pedal is at the lowest point.
- Start slowly with little resistance.
- In the beginning, do not pedal faster than 15 to 20 miles per hour, or 60 revolutions per minute.
- Before you add resistance to the cycle, make sure that you have warmed up for 5 minutes

KEY FORMULAS

Momentum = Mass x Velocity

Acceleration = $\dfrac{\text{Change in Velocity}}{\text{Total Time}}$

Speed = $\dfrac{\text{Distance}}{\text{Time}}$

Work=Force x Distance

Power= $\dfrac{\text{F x D}}{\text{T}}$

Karvonen Formula
Using the Karvonen formula, the generally accepted heart-rate ranges are between 60% to 80% of maximal heart-rate reserve.
Target heart-rate = % intensity X heart-rate reserve + resting heart-rate

Maximal Heart-Rate Formula
Maximal heart-rate formula is the standard that was used in most group exercise settings:
target heart-rate = maximal heart-rate (mhr) X % intensity

HEART RATE

You can take a client's pulse at two different places. The wrist pulse is located at the base of either thumb. Place the finger pads (not the tips) of two or three fingers of the opposite hand on the base of the thumb. Do not press the artery too hard as it will constrict the artery and it cannot be felt. A light but firm pressure will allow you to feel it well.

The carotid pulse is located on either side of your windpipe. It is one of the easiest arteries to feel because it is one of the largest. Use the right middle fingers to feel the left carotid or the left middle fingers to feel the right artery. Do not press both carotid arteries at the same time as this may cause you to faint or feel lighthearted. Be careful when pressing near the jawbone as this can stimulate sensitive nerves and cause you to feel faint. To be on safe side, feel only one artery at a time.

Target heart rate zone is the predermined range of beats per minute, used to monitor training intensity. The ACSM recommends the intensity of exercise be prescribed as 55 to 90% of maxiumum heart rate, or 50 to 85% of VO2 max or HR reserve. However, individuals with a very low initial level of fitness may benefit from training intensities as low as 40% to 50% of VO2 max. The following are the primary methods of calculating Target Heart Rate:

The formula for obtaining 55 to 90% maximum heart rate (HRmax) equals 220 minus your age x 55% to 90%.

FITNESS TIPS

Fitness Misconceptions

No pain, no gain
Pain happens to be the body's signal that something is amiss. Stop the activity because serious injury may occur to the body part in pain.

Excessive sweating means that you are out of shape.
Just the opposite is usually true. The more fit an individual is, the better the body is at cooling itself.

Drinking water during exercise gives an individual cramps.
According to doctors, an individual should drink water before, during, and after exercise. This prevents dehydration and overheating.

If an individual stops exercising, muscle will turn to fat.
Since the make-up of muscle cells and fat cells are different, this is impossible. What actually happens is that muscles shrink and fat accrues because fewer calories are burned.

An individual should eat lots of protein when exercising a lot. Proteins are the building blocks of muscles. Working out requires extra energy, which is best gained from carbohydrates followed by protein after working out.

EXERCISE IN THE USA

Approximately 25% of adults in the United States do not engage in any leisure-time physical activity and, of those that do, only about 20% engage in regular, sustained leisure-time physical activity. The Surgeon General's Report on Health and Physical Activity contains public health recommendations that now endorse moderate as well as vigorous levels of physical activity for achieving cardiorespiratory fitness . People who are inactive can significantly improve their health and well-being by participating in moderate levels of physical activity on a regular basis while even greater health benefits can be attained by regular participation in more vigorous physical activity.

Cardiorespiratory endurance is considered an important health-related component of physical fitness which can reduce the morbidity and mortality risks associated with some of the leading causes of illness and death in the United States. The goal, then, is to guide individuals to moderate to vigorous intensity exercise conducive to achieving the most health and fitness benefits for their time invested. Heart rate (HR) is considered the standard for estimating exercise training intensity in the field based on its linear relationship to VO2. The recommendations of the American College of Sports Medicine (ACSM) for moderate to hard relative exercise training intensities for cardiorespiratory fitness based on HR are 55%-90% of maximum heart rate (HRmax) or 40%-85% of heart rate reserve (HRR).

To be effective, an accurate determination of HR must be obtained, often requiring individuals to stop their activity temporarily to palpate their pulse rate. In addition, many individuals experience difficulty palpating a pulse or accurately timing their pulse count which can result in subject error. It has been suggested that individuals who use HR to monitor their exercise intensity may become overly preoccupied with the monitoring of their HR in order to avoid deviating from their targeted training range. This preoccupation and frequent pauses in activity to obtain an accurate heart rate are believed to have a negative effect on activity enjoyment and long-term compliance. Use of a heart rate monitor would eliminate many of the problems associated with palpating a pulse and would provide an alternative means by which an individual could use HR as a guide to estimating exercise intensity. However, some individuals may perceive the need to wear a device during exercise as bothersome or the additional expense of a HR monitor a barrier to initiating an exercise regimen.

Another method advocated for prescribing an exercise training intensity is based on the talk test method or ability of an individual to carry on a conversation during exercise; the counting talk test. The rationale for this method is based on the premise that exercising at or above the ventilatory threshold generally does not allow complete conversational sentences without pausing for breaths and thus serves well as a means of estimating the ceiling training intensity (6). The main advantage of this method is its simplicity of use. Recently it has been shown that when using the talk test method to estimate exercise intensity, individuals exercised at 85-88% of HRmax at the maximal point at which they could speak comfortably or were equivocal in their response. When subjects could no longer speak comfortably their exercise intensity was greater than the 90% HRmax limit
advocated by the ACSM. Though the talk test method is effective for defining an upper limit of exercise intensity for cardiorespiratory training, it does not provide adequate feedback as to

lower levels of exercise intensity that produce cardiorespiratory fitness. This is caused by the ability to converse comfortably in complete sentences when exercise at intensities that range from rest to this "ceiling intensity".

CLIENT CONSULTATION—

ASSESSMENT; EVALUATION TESTS; FORMS

STEPS TO TAKE IN EVALUATING A CASE STUDY OR A POTENTIAL CLIENT:
1. Determine the number of cardiovascular disease risk factors.
2. Determine if the client has any symptoms of cardiovascular, pulmonary or metabolic disease.
3. Evaluate the client's level of risk according to the American College of Sports Medicine's guidelines
4. Determine whether the client should receive a medical clearance from a physician. Use the ACSM standards and any other justifications.
5. Determine whether the client should take a fitness test.
6. If a fitness test is taken, assess the results.
7. Evaluate the client's goals, interests and enthusiasm.
8. Develop a wellness plan based on all available information.
9. Determine when the client should take another fitness test.
10. Suggest changes to the lifestyle according to the client's needs.

STANDARD FITNESS ASSESSMENT:
The order of the assessment is important in that resting components will be difficult to assess after activity has begun, and muscular activity will increase cardiovascular activity.
1. Check heart rate and blood pressure at rest —
   Ideally the resting heart rate will be most accurate if the client measures his or her heart rate before rising in the morning on three mornings, and taking an average of the measurements. If this is not possible, have the client rest for 5 minutes before testing.
2. Check body measurements (weight, abdominal and hip measurements)
3. Cardiovascular fitness tests
4. Test muscular strength and endurance
5. Check flexibility
6. Perform any other needed tests.

CRITERIA—ACCEPT CLIENT? REQUIRE MEDICAL CLEARANCE? REFER?
If a potential client has two or more risk factors or symptoms of diseases of the heart, blood vessels, lungs or metabolism, or been diagnosed with any of these diseases, the client should receive clearance from a medical doctor before being accepted as a client. Pregnant women, men over age 45 and women over age 55 should receive a clearance from a medical doctor. Anyone with chronic conditions such as asthma should receive clearance from a medical doctor, as well as anyone who has recently suffered an injury or been admitted to a hospital. Potential clients taking prescription medications should disclose these so that the trainer can discuss the

potential effects on exercise with the physician. A trainer should be realistic about his or her own level of skill and knowledge, and should refer anyone whom is determined to be risky to a physician or a more skilled fitness trainer.

FORMS—MEDICAL HISTORY (ITS IMPORTANCE TO PFT):

A medical history form is a questionnaire designed to elicit information from a client regarding his or her health status. A well-written form will ask for information about risk factors for a variety of health problems, including information about age, genetic health history, weight, cholesterol levels, and blood glucose levels, as well as behavioral risk factors including smoking history and activity levels. After reviewing the medical history form, a personal trainer must determine whether he or she will agree to take the person as a client, may require a medical clearance from a medical doctor before agreeing to take the person as a client, or may refuse to accept that person as a client and instead refer them to a medical program for more appropriate program.

FORMS—IN ADDITION TO MEDICAL CLEARANCE, PT SHOULD CONSIDER ADMINISTERING PRIOR TO BEGINNING TRAINING PROGRAM:

- The *Physical Activity Readiness Questionnaire* (PAR-Q) elicits information about a client's health history, but should be used in conjunction with a medical history form in order to assess cardiovascular health risks.
- The *informed consent form* notifies clients of possible hazards of beginning an exercise program.
- The *agreement and release of liability form* as signed by the client may discharge the trainer from some liability in the case of injury or harm received by entering into an activity plan.
- The *exercise and activity quiz* gives data about a client's activity habits, goals, and attitudes toward exercise and can help begin a conversation with the trainer about the reasons for seeing a personal fitness trainer.
- The *nutrition and weight profile* can give the trainer information about a client's food intake, but can also provide the client with some information about his or her own diet.
- The *self-assessment quiz* is a tool for educating and motivating the client about the importance of a healthy lifestyle.

Client's History

The first step in the preparticipation evaluation is to assess for contraindications to exercise testing and training and to identify any risks or limitations relevant to the exercise prescription. An efficient screening questionnaire addresses previous exercise programs; present activity (frequency, duration, and intensity); existing chronic or acute disease(s), especially chronic obstructive pulmonary disease, cardiovascular disease, and extreme motor limitations because of severe arthritis; family history of cardiorespiratory disease; and coronary artery disease risk factors. The history should also include a current systems review, risk factors that are possibly modifiable through exercise, and a medication review to determine any potential interaction with exercise testing or training.

TABLE 1. Patient Profile and History   Date: _____

Name: _____

Address: _____

Telephone _____ Age: _____ Weight: _____

Percent fat: _____ Lean mass in lb: _____

Goals: _____

Risk factors (circle):
        Family History
        Diabetes
        Sedentary
        Hyperlipidemia
        Hypertension
        Stress
        Smoker (Quit___)
        Other

Limitations (circle):
        Asthma
        Osteoporosis
        Arthritis
        Recent surgery
        Menopausal
        Menstrual irregularity
        Heart disease

Orthopedic (circle):
        Low back
        Knees
        Shoulder

Other/additional information: _____

Medications:

Type:_____ Function:_____

Type:_____ Function:_____

Type:_____ Function:_____

Type:_____ Function:_____

Equipment Available:

Home: _____

Club: _____

Work: _____

Sports: _____

Current Exercise Program:

Cardiovascular Types:_____

Frequency:_____

Duration:_____

Intensity:_____

Strength

Types: _____

Frequency: _____

Sets: _____

Reps: _____

To failure?: _____

Flexibility: _____

Summary and recommendations: _____

Physician: _____

TESTS

TESTS FOR ASSESSING CARDIORESPIRATORY FITNESS:

1. A diagnostic exercise test uses an EKG machine to determine if a person exercising as hard as he or she can.
2. A functional maximal exercise test involves exercising as hard as he or she can, and measuring the oxygen used.
3. A submaximal exercise test involves a person exercising to a particular level of activity (often 85% of the estimated maximum heart rate) or for a particular length of time:
   - Multi-stage submaximal tests involve exercising at different intensities for a certain amount of time and then measuring the body's reactions after each stage.
   - Single-stage submaximal tests have the person do one activity at one intensity for a period of time and then and then measuring the body's reactions after the test.
4. The 3-minute YMCA step test measures how quickly the heart rate recovers from moderate exercise.
5. The Rockport Walking Test measures heart rate after walking a mile briskly.

TESTS FOR DETERMINING STRENGTH AND EDURANCE OF LARGE MUSCLE GROUPS:

- **Static (isometric) tests** check the muscle's ability to resist a force while staying
- in a certain position and dynamic (isotonic) tests check the muscle's ability to move a force.
- A **dynamometer** is a device that measures the force of a muscle contraction at a particular muscle position.
- The **one-repetition maximum test** (1RM) assesses strength in motion by having the person perform an exercise one time with the maximum amount of weight he or she can tolerate.
- Tests to determine muscular **endurance** include:
    - ✓ The **push-up test** measures how many times a person can push the upper body up from a prone position.
    - ✓ The **dynamic bench press test** in which a person lifts a standardized weight at a particular rhythm for as many repetitions as he or she can.
    - ✓ The **sit-up test** tests the number of abdominal curls in one minute.

TESTS FOR MEASURING FLEXIBILITY AND POSTURE:

- The sit and reach test has person sit with feet flexed in front and reach toward the toes, keeping the legs straight.
- The trunk extension ability test requires the person to push himself up from a face-down position while keeping the hips on the floor.
- Hamstring flexibility is measured by the person lying on her back and lifting one leg in the air.
- Hip flexor flexibility is measured by lying on the back and pulling the knee into the chest.
- Quadriceps flexibility is measured by lying face-down and pulling the heel toward the buttocks.
- Calf flexibility is measured by flexing the foot while standing with the back against a wall.
- Shoulder flexibility is measured by lying on the back and reaching the arms overhead or by reaching the hands together behind the back with one arm reaching back over the shoulder and the other reaching up under the arm.

Testing Flexibility

Flexibility can be measured by the sit-and-reach test and range-of-motion assessment. Agility can be determined by asking the patient to walk a heel-to-toe balance line.

	Yardstick Position (in.)	
Flexibility Level	Age 50-59	Age 60+
	Men	
High	16+	15+
Average	10-15	9-14
Below average	7-9	6-8
Low	6	5

Women		
High	19+	18+
Average	13-18	12-17
Below average	10-12	9-11
Low	9	8

Lipid levels

A fasting lipid profile to measure total cholesterol, high-density and low-density lipoprotein subfractions, and triglycerides can provide a baseline for the sedentary patient to assess exercise benefits.

PROGRAM PLANNING

ORDER OF EXERCISES

The order of the exercise will affect the severity of the workout. The order will develop the basic framework for the workout. Basic questions to ask:
1. Does your client's workout need to progress from upper to lower body or vice-versa?
2. Does your client's workout progress from body part (small muscle group) to structural (large muscle group) or just the opposite?

The classical exercise order is from upper body to lower, and large muscle group to small. Order your client's exercise program based on their athletic training level. If the client is a beginner, start with a less severe workout order; use an upper to lower body progression.

AGE CONSIDERATIONS—GUIDELINES FOR PLANNING ACTIVITIES

CONSIDERATIONS AND BENEFITS FOR PEOPLE OVER 65 IN EXERCISE PROGRAMS:
Older people may come to a new exercise program with certain problems:
- The blood vessels may be less elastic and the heart fills with blood slower, so the heart cannot beat as fast as in younger people.
- Older adults use oxygen less efficiently.
- Blood pressure may be higher.
- Older adults may use more medicines.
- Reflexes and reactions are slower.
- Risk of having weaker, porous bones and the disintegration of cartilage, making knee and back injuries more likely.
- Higher body fat and less strength in the muscles
- Stiff joints and higher risk of injury.

- Reduced working of the kidneys, so possibility of dehydration.

The **benefits** of exercise for older adults are:

Stronger muscles, lower loss of bone, improved flexibility and movement, better poise and less risk for falling, better use of oxygen, lower body fat, better use of insulin and glucose, and less risk of atherosclerosis.

PLANNING TRAINING PROGRAM FOR OLDER ADULT—THINGS TO REMEMBER:

✓ Be sure the person is cleared by a doctor before beginning any program.

✓ When testing fitness, make sure to use age-appropriate standards.

✓ As with all people, remember that some elderly people will be highly unfit, while others may be very fit, with every stage in between.

✓ Begin slowly and progress slowly.

✓ Warm up and cool down for longer periods.

✓ For those who are weak or inflexible, avoid weight-bearing activities. For those without such problems, begin weight training slowly.

✓ Moderate the workout if arthritis pain occurs.

✓ Most elderly people should focus on activities that will make daily tasks easier, focusing on flexibility exercises.

✓ Work with the physician to get recommendations for the intensity of the workout.

✓ The primary goal should be to motivate the person to exercise for life, so notice anything that may demotivate them, such as pain, doing too much, or engaging in activities the person doesn't like.

PLANNING TRAINING ACTIVITY PROGRAM FOR CHILDREN UNDER 12—GUIDELINES:

✓ Children should be active throughout the day, not sitting for more than 2 hours.

✓ Activities should be right for the age of the child. As they get older, they should do a more extended 30+-minute activity on most days.

✓ Children should be active for at least an hour a day total, and having many short-term activities (15 minutes) throughout the day is ideal.

✓ Weight training should be moderate and children should not try to compete with each other for lifting weights.

✓ Because they are more likely to overheat, be sure children drink a lot of water and do not stay in the heat too long while doing an activity.

HEALTH CONSIDERATIONS—GUIDELINES FOR PLANNING ACTIVITIES; HIGH-RISK CLIENTS

SYMPTOMS/CONDITIONS INDICATIVE OF DISEASES THAT REQUIRE MEDICAL CLEARANCE PRIOR TO EXERCISE PROGRAM; LOW-, MODERATE-, HIGH-RISK CLIENTS AS DEFINED BY THE AMERICAN COLLEGE OF SPORTS MEDICINE:

Symptoms which indicate to a personal fitness trainer that a potential client should receive clearance from a medical doctor prior to starting an exercise program:

- Angina - pain in the chest, arm, neck or jaw
- Dyspnea - difficulty breathing while resting or sleeping
- Syncope - dizziness or fainting
- Edema - swelling of the ankles
- Unusual or uneven heartbeat.

- Leg or foot cramps when performing an activity.
- Heart murmur
- Any exhaustion or difficulty breathing during normal behavior.

Low-risk clients are men under the age of 45 or women under the age of 55 who have no symptoms of cardiovascular, pulmonary or metabolic disease and one or fewer risk factors. **Moderate-risk clients** are men at or above age 45 or women at or above age 55, or anyone of any age with two risk factors. **High-risk clients** are anyone with symptoms or diagnosis of diseases of the heart, blood vessels, lungs or metabolism.

CHD and CVD; RISK FACTORS:

CHD, or **coronary heart disease**, also called **coronary artery disease (CAD)**, is one of the diseases classified as **cardiovascular disease (CVD)**. Cardiovascular disease causes more deaths than any other diseases in the United States and the Western world. Cardiovascular disease is any of a number of conditions in which blood flow to the heart and through the blood vessels is impeded. CHD is usually the result of **atherosclerosis**, which describes the inside of the blood vessels becoming smaller due to hard deposits forming inside of the vessels. Heredity and age are strong risk factors for CHD that cannot be altered. However, risk factors such as smoking, high blood pressure, high cholesterol levels in the blood, high blood sugar, excess body fat, and a lack of physical activity can often be modified through behavior change in order to reduce the risk of CHD and CVD.

CVD—OTHER CONDITIONS WHICH CAN RESULT:

- Myocardial ischemia is a condition in which not enough blood gets to the heart muscle.
- Myocardial infarction, also called MI or heart attack, occurs when blood stops going to the heart, caused by an artery bringing blood to the heart getting completely clogged. Parts of the heart muscle that do not receive blood may die.
- Angina pectoris is chest pain caused by coronary heart disease. Stable angina can be expected at certain times in people with CHD, such as during exercise, but will go away at other times. Unstable angina is unexpected and happens when the person is resting. Anyone experiencing unstable angina is at risk for a heart attack and should seek medical care immediately.
- Stroke is a sudden clog of blood to the brain. Parts of the brain that do not receive adequate blood may die.

CVD—RISK FACTORS CITED BY THE AMERICAN COLLEGE OF SPORTS MEDICINE:

1. Genetic history, particularly a parent who experienced a heart attack, coronary bypass surgery (cardiac revascularization) or sudden death at a young age (mother under age 65 or father under age 55).
2. A current or recent smoker (within the past 6 months).
3. High blood pressure, specifically a systolic pressure at or over 140 mmHg or a diastolic pressure at or over 90 mmHg, or being treated for hypertension.
4. High cholesterol levels (dyslipidemia) with the LDL level over 130 mg/dl or the HDL level under 40 mg/dl or being treated for high cholesterol
5. High blood glucose of 100 mg/dl or above after fasting.
6. Excess body fat, determined by body mass index above 30, abdominal measurement of over 102 cm in men and 88 cm in women, or waist-to-hip ratio of .95 or above for men or .86 or above for women.
7. Inactivity or low activity.

METABOLIC SYNDROME—RISKS; ROLE OF A PERSONAL TRAINER:
Metabolic Syndrome is defined as the presence of several diseases that are precursors to diabetes and/or cardiovascular disease. Specifically, a person with increased systolic or diastolic blood pressure, excess insulin, high levels of sugar in the blood, high cholesterol or who is overweight (especially those with too much abdominal fat) may be diagnosed with Metabolic Syndrome. Someone diagnosed with Metabolic Syndrome will most likely be advised by a doctor to lose weight, eat a diet low in fat and high in fiber, and begin an exercise program. A personal trainer can guide a person in developing an exercise routine that the person can stick to. The personal trainer can also suggest ways to stick to a diet and encourage the person in losing weight.

THREE TYPES OF ARTHRITIS—HOW THEY MAY AFFECT A TRAINING PROGRAM:
1. *Osteoarthritis* affects many adults, commonly in the knee and hand. The cartilage disintegrates, leaving the bones to rub against one another and cause damage. Symptoms include stiffness and pain. Pain may come and go, so workouts should be done on days of lower pain. Exercise has been shown to relieve symptoms. Exercise programs should focus on flexibility and lower intensity, isometric exercises.
2. *Rheumatoid arthritis* is a swelling of the tissues around the joints and is found usually in the hands, feet and wrists. Exercise can help increase flexibility and movement and reduce pain, but due to its severity, people with rheumatoid arthritis should see a medical professional for exercise programs.
3. *Fibromyalgia* is an overall pain in the area of most joints, accompanied by extreme tiredness, inability to sleep, and irritable bowel syndrome. Cardio exercises may help reduce pain, but doing too much can make the pain worse, so start slowly.

OSTEOPOROSIS—THINGS TO CONSIDER WHEN WORKING WITH A CLIENT:
Osteoporosis is a condition seen in older people in which the bones become more porous and less dense. Possible causes include inadequate amounts of vitamin D and/or calcium, lack of activity, smoking, and drinking larger amounts of alcohol. Smaller, lighter women who are inactive are most susceptible.
- ✓ People with low bone density should not curve the back, but remain standing up as much as possible.
- ✓ Extending the back (bending backward) may be helpful.
- ✓ Doing weight-bearing exercises along with cardio activities four days a week, weight training alone twice a week, and flexibility exercises daily is the best method of improvement.
- ✓ Repeat the activity more often with less weight.
- ✓ Stick to lower impact activities.

BLOOD PRESSURE—SYSTOLIC PRESSURE, DIASTOLIC PRESSURE AND HYPERTENSION:
Blood pressure is the force of the blood inside the arteries as it pushes against the artery walls. *Systolic pressure* is the force inside the arteries during a heartbeat, when blood is being forced through the arteries. *Diastolic pressure* is the force inside the arteries in between heartbeats, when blood is not being forced through the arteries (although blood always fills the arteries, just with less force in between beats). *Hypertension* is blood pressure elevated above 140 mmHg of systolic pressure and/or 90mmHg diastolic pressure. Hypertension is a risk factor for coronary heart disease because it is often caused by the arteries becoming clogged with deposits, making the heart work harder and apply more force to push the blood through the constricted tubes of the arteries.

HIGH BLOOD PRESSURE—GUIDELINES FOR PLANNING CLIENT ACTIVITIES:
- ✓ If state law allows, take blood pressure at the beginning, middle and end of activity.
- ✓ Be sure to refer particularly ill people to medical professionals, including those whose systolic pressure is over 160 and diastolic pressure is over 90 or whose blood pressure goes down when exercising.
- ✓ Watch for signs of heart attack or stroke.
- ✓ Limit the intensity of the activity to moderate to low.
- ✓ Be aware of how the person's medications may affect the person's exercise program.
- ✓ Those with high blood pressure should be careful when doing weight training, making sure to avoid too-heavy weights and too much tension in muscles.
- ✓ Avoid holding the breath or closing the throat (Valsalva maneuver).
- ✓ Keep the feet below the head.

STROKE—GUIDELINES FOR PLANNING CLIENT ACTIVITIES:
People who have had a stroke should be cleared by a doctor before starting an exercise program. They may not be able to see well, may have weak muscles, may not be able to feel touch on some areas, or may have lost mental capabilities, causing them to forget things or have difficulty understanding instructions. Because their ability to maintain balance is impaired, people who have had a stroke should do more stationary, seated cardio activities, like the exercise bike.
- ✓ If lifting weights, use weight machines rather than free weights whenever possible.
- ✓ Focus on exercises to increase balance.
- ✓ Watch for signs of heart attack or stroke.
- ✓ Limit the intensity of the activity to moderate to low.
- ✓ Be aware of how the person's medications may affect the person's exercise program.
- ✓ Avoid holding the breath or closing the throat (Valsalva maneuver).
- ✓ Keep the feet below the head.

DIABETES—GUIDELINES FOR PLANNING CLIENT ACTIVITIES:
People with diabetes must be cleared by a doctor for exercise.
- ✓ Look for a sudden drop in blood sugar, which requires immediate medical intervention. Keep sugar on hand and know the symptoms of low blood sugar, including tiredness, feeling nauseated, dizzy or faint, sweating a lot, headaches, being confused, or a sudden increase in the heart beat.
- ✓ Be sure that those who take insulin have discussed with their doctor the proper dosage of insulin when beginning an exercise program, and do not exercise muscles where insulin was injected for at least one hour.
- ✓ The person should eat foods high in carbohydrates before activities, and also during long periods of exertion.
- ✓ Cardio activities using at least 1000 calories per week is recommended.
- ✓ Remind people to watch their feet for injuries and to keep the feet clean and healthy, since diabetes can damage nerves and blood vessels in the feet.

COPD—GUIDELINES FOR PLANNING CLIENT ACTIVITIES:
- ✓ COPD (Chronic Obstructive Pulmonary Disease), including chronic bronchitis, asthma and emphysema, is a diagnosis in which the lungs are reduced in function. Only those with mild COPD should see a trainer without being in a medically supervised program.
- ✓ The best activity is walking.
- ✓ Have the person identify his or her own level of discomfort or shortness of breath during the activity.

- ✓ When beginning the program, the length of the exercise may be very short, only a few minutes.
- ✓ Weight training for the upper body is recommended.
- ✓ Work the muscles of breathing and do not tilt the upper body downward if it causes difficulty breathing.

ASTHMA—EXERCISE INDUCED; ANY TYPE—GUIDELINES FOR PLANNING CLIENT ACTIVITIES:

Exercise induced asthma (EIA) is a milder form of asthma in which beginning an activity brings on an asthma attack in which the person cannot breathe well and will cough and wheeze. However, once the incident is over, it will not recur for 1-4 hours afterward. Some athletes will use this factor to induce an attack during a warm up period so as to avoid one during competition.

When planning activities for people with asthma:
- ✓ Be sure to have client perform longer warm ups.
- ✓ Avoid dry, cold air.
- ✓ Keep the intensity of the activity moderate and short.
- ✓ Brief spurts of activity will be less likely to induce an asthma attack.
- ✓ Encourage client to avoid breathing through the mouth too much.
- ✓ Remind client to take medications as prescribed, including any preventatives and preventative use of emergency inhalers.

CANCER; PERIPHERAL VASCULAR DISEASE—GUIDELINES FOR PLANNING CLIENT ACTIVITIES:
- ✓ Note whether the person has any complications or other conditions that may affect training.
- ✓ Be aware of the stage the cancer is in and what type of treatment he or she is getting.
- ✓ Do only lower to medium intensity activities.
- ✓ Reduce exposure to bacteria or any activity that is more likely to cause injury.
- ✓ Do not do exercises that may weaken or break bones that are painful or infused with cancer.

Peripheral vascular disease (PVD) is when the blood vessels in the limbs are hardened and starting to be blocked. As the blood works harder to reach the arms and legs, a pain called claudication happens.
- ✓ Work with the doctor to design an appropriate program
- ✓ Warm ups and cool downs should be longer, at least 5-10 minutes.
- ✓ Ideally, walking in brief spurts with frequent rest periods is best for reducing pain.

NEUROMUSCULAR DISORDERS—GUIDELINES FOR PLANNING CLIENT ACTIVITIES:
- ▪ For people with **multiple sclerosis**, consider planning activities that reduce the chance that the person will lose his balance, such as chair aerobics, using a stationary bicycle, weight machines, swimming or water aerobics. Also be sure the environment is cooler because people with MS tend to feel hot more than others. Weight training is recommended for helping with daily tasks.
- ▪ For people with **Parkinson's disease**, also plan activities that reduce the chance the person will lose her balance. In addition, work the erector spinae, middle trapezius, rhomboids, gluteus maximus, and gastrocnemius in order to improve posture and prevent leaning forward too much. Stretching and plyometric activities may help increase mobility and help in performing daily tasks.

PREGNANCY CONSIDERATIONS

EFFECTS PREGNANCY CAN HAVE ON BODY, WHICH MAY AFFECT TRAINING ACTIVITIES:
- ✓ Stress on the hips and lower back, along with a higher risk of falling.
- ✓ Nerve pain due to swelling, such as carpal tunnel syndrome.
- ✓ Increased amounts of blood.
- ✓ Faster rate of heartbeat and higher blood pressure
- ✓ Pressure from the uterus on the blood vessel running to the heart from the legs
- ✓ Less room for the diaphragm, so some difficulty breathing may occur
- ✓ Increase in the diameter of the ribcage
- ✓ Higher metabolism and warmer body temperature (but less ability to stand heat)
- ✓ Feeling tired and sick
- ✓ Separation of the muscles in the abdomen
- ✓ Increased flexibility of the tissues around joints
- ✓ Digestive problems
- ✓ Insomnia
- ✓ Increased emotional sensitivity
- ✓ Increased likelihood of varicose veins

BENEFITS AND RISKS OF EXERCISE DURING PREGNANCY:
The **benefits** of exercise during pregnancy include better blood flow, sleep patterns and digestion. Women also may have a better ability to bear their increased weight due to stronger muscles, may feel more lively, fewer back and muscle pains, and gaining less weight. Pregnant women who stay active are less likely to contract gestational diabetes and pregnancy-induced hypertension (PIH). The **risks and concerns** of exercise for pregnant women include not gaining enough weight and thus restricting the growth of the fetus, too-high body temperature which may lead to birth defects, possible redirection of the blood flow or glucose away from the fetus during exercise. In general, however, most women should consider an exercise program during pregnancy.

REASONS SOME WOMEN SHOULD NOT EXERCISE DURING PREGNANCY:
Women who should not exercise during pregnancy without a doctor's clearance include those who:
- ✓ have very low levels of iron in the blood;
- ✓ have a heart murmur;
- ✓ have chronic bronchitis;
- ✓ have type 1 diabetes;
- ✓ have high blood pressure that is not well-managed;
- ✓ have a diagnosis of intrauterine growth restriction;
- ✓ are very overweight or underweight;
- ✓ smoke;
- ✓ have seizures;
- ✓ have overactive thyroid.

Some women should **definitely not** exercise during pregnancy:
- ✓ if they have a diagnosis of heart or lung disease,
- ✓ if they have a cervix that will not stay closed,
- ✓ are carrying more than one baby,
- ✓ are at risk for pre-term labor,

✓ have had bleeding in the last 2 trimesters,
✓ have been diagnosed with placenta previa after week 26 of the pregnancy,
✓ have a broken bag of waters, or a diagnosis of PIH.

AMERICAN COLLEGE OF OBSTETRICIANS and GYNECOLOGISTS' RECOMMENDATIONS FOR EXERCISING DURING PREGNANCY:

- Most pregnant women should exercise for at least 30 minutes a day of medium intensity exercise.
- Avoid exercises in which the risk of injury is high, including activities in which the belly is at risk, or any activities at very low or very high elevations.
- If beginning an activity program for the first time, the best method is to begin in the second trimester with a very low intensity workout.
- Women should listen to their bodies and not do more than they feel they should.
- Drink extra water during activity.
- Progression is not necessary during pregnancy, only that the woman maintains a level of fitness rather than increasing her activity level over the course of the pregnancy.
- Stop exercising if vaginal bleeding begins, the fetal movements decline, if you are feeling faint, if the bag of waters breaks or leaks, or if contractions begin.

INJURIES; RISKS; GUIDELINES FOR REDUCING INJURY

WHY INJURIES OCCUR:
Every effort must be taken to insure that the client is not injured during strengthening activities. Injuries occur for a variety of reasons, some that you can control and some that cannot be controlled by you. Clients have different levels of abilities. Some are limited in the basic components of physical and skills fitness. Some are limited by their attitudes. Some are limited by their disabilities. Be diligent in understanding your client's level of fitness so that injuries can be avoided.

COMMON FITNESS INJURIES:
A bruise is an injury that may occur during physical activities. It is an injury to the skin that comes from being hit, pushed, or squeezed. Bruises can occur anywhere on the body, and the area is usually sore, swollen and often red or blue in color. Most bruises will heal in 3 to 10 days on their own. Bruises do not usually produce any serious medical problems. A few bruises can be very serious. For example, infection can develop in the bruised area, internal injuries to the liver, lungs, heart or brain can occur, and extreme swelling can cut off circulation to the extremity.

A muscle cramp or "charley horse" is very painful and frightening for the exerciser. It becomes very incapacitating. When a client suffers from a muscle cramp, do the following:
1. Massage the muscle.
2. Try to straighten the affected limb.
3. Drink water to re-hydrate the muscles as cramps usually occur during prolonged and vigorous exercise.
4. Take a break.

A broken bone is another hazard of physical activities. The human body has approximately 206 bones that form the skeleton. Attached to these bones are a variety of muscles and soft tissues. There are two basic types of broken bones. In a compound fracture, the broken ends of the bone are out of alignment and a segment of the bone may emerge through the soft tissue and skin. A simple fracture breaks through the bone but does not displace the bone sections. If the exerciser has received a severe blow to a body part, complains of pain or tenderness to the touch, can not use or move a body part, or has swelling and discoloration, think broken or fractured bone. The client should not move if he/she appears to have a broken or fractured bone. If possible, lie down and cover yourself to prevent shock. Seek medical attention immediately. Tenderness in a specific location can be the key indicator of a fracture, but this is not always the case.

Blisters are a troubling part of the exercise program. They can occur on the feet and the hands. Blisters form when the skin rubs against another surface. A tear occurs under the upper layers of the skin causing a space to form between the layers of the skin while leaving the surface intact. Fluid seeps into the space and thus, you have a very painful injury, a blister. Ill fitting shoes and moisture are usually the culprit.

Dehydration is the loss of water and important blood salts like potassium and sodium. Some early warning signs of dehydration include mild to severe thirst, dry lips, and a rapid, weak pulse. In severe cases, a person develops cold hands and feet, blue lips, and confusion. To avoid dehydration, drink adequate water before and after physical activities. If symptoms appear severe, seek medical attention immediately.

Heat stress and heat stroke are the loss of body fluids through increased perspiration with an elevated body temperature. Symptoms include decreased sweating, muscle cramps, increased heat rate, or lightheadedness. If symptoms are mild, remove yourself to a shady spot and get plenty of fluids. If symptoms appear severe, seek medical attention immediately. Both of these conditions can be avoided by being aware of how your body feels and to drink fluids frequently. Don't wait until you feel thirsty to drink fluids. Don't ignore the warning signals of dehydration. It is important to replace water lost through sweating because it helps to keep your body temperature down. It also helps to hydrate the skin and muscles. Just how much water should you drink? Drink at least one 8 ounce glass of water before you start, sip frequently during the work out, and drink at least two glasses after the exercise routine.

In general, stop strength training if your client experiences any of the following:
- Chest pain, pain in the neck, teeth, arms, or jaw
- Dizziness
- Excessive fatigue
- Headache
- Irregularity of your pulse
- Light-headedness
- Nausea and/or vomiting
- Shortness of breath
- Any unusual joint, muscle, or ligament problems

MOST COMMON REASONS SOME PEOPLE ARE MORE LIKELY TO BE INJURED; GENERAL GUIDELINES FOR REDUCING INJURY:
✓ Having some muscles much stronger than others

- ✓ Genetic bone configuration making some injuries more likely
- ✓ Past damage to the body
- ✓ Being overweight
- ✓ Having excessively long tendons allowing the joints to stretch more than normal
- ✓ Sickness or disease
- ✓ Legs of different lengths
- ✓ General lack of flexibility
- ✓ Not warming up prior to exercise
- ✓ Doing activities too fast
- ✓ Getting tired
- ✓ Repeating an activity too many times in a row
- ✓ Working too hard (i.e. lifting too much weight or running too fast)
- ✓ Doing activity improperly or in the wrong position
- ✓ Wearing the wrong shoes
- ✓ Dangerous surroundings (weather, broken equipment, etc.)
- ✓ Weak torso muscles
- ✓ Mistaking injured limbs for normal soreness

To reduce injury, the person should start an activity at a lower level of difficulty for themselves, and then increase the workload slowly after 2-3 weeks at one level. Workouts that are too long, too intense, or occur too frequently increase the risk of injury.

ACUTE INJURY; CHRONIC INJURY; MUSCLE STRAIN; SPRAIN; SUBLUXATION; DISLOCATION; TENDINITIS; SYNOVITIS:

- *Acute injury* is damage to the body that happens because of a sudden problem in the body's alignment.
- A *chronic injury* is damage that is done to the body over time (such as repeated acute injuries).
- A *muscle strain* is minor damage to a connective tissue or muscle.
- A *sprain* is more severe damage to a connective tissue.
- *Subluxation* happens when a joint is partly separated and the connective tissues around the joint are then stretched or damaged.
- *Dislocation* is the separation of the bones of a joint.
- *Tendinitis* is a chronic condition in which a tendon is damaged due to stress over time and then swells, which causes scars and calcium deposits to form.
- *Synovitis* is the swelling of the synovial membrane, which holds synovial fluid, and acts as a cushion. Synovial membranes are found in between major joints such as the shoulder, elbow and knee.

BURSITIS; CONTUSION; ADHESIONS; CONTRACTURES and JOINT DYSFUNCTION:

- *Bursitis* is inflammation of the fluid-filled sac (bursa) that cushions the space between the bone and a tendon.
- A *contusion* is damage to tissue in which blood vessels are damaged and blood leaks into the tissue, swelling the area (also called a bruise).
- *Adhesions* are clumps of collagen attaching to tissue after it is injured. This reduces the flexibility.
- A *contracture* is excessive tension in a tissue (skin, muscle, connecting tissue, etc.) that makes it impossible to move normally.
- *Joint dysfunction* is the lack of normal movement in a joint that can be painful, caused by misalignment, injury, lack of use, or old age.

THREE STAGES OF INFLAMMATION AND REPAIR:

1. Acute (inflammatory) stage – Immediately after being injured, the area will be painful and swell, get red and hot, and may feel stiff.
2. Subacute (repair and healing) stage – About a week after the injury, the damage begins to be fixed, new tissues are made, which are easily damaged if overused. Scar tissue is prominently featured in the new tissue. Swelling lessens.
3. Chronic (maturation and remodeling) stage – A few weeks after the injury, the injury is mostly healed, but scar tissue continues to form in the damaged area and the new tissue gets stronger. As this happens, the area may be weaker than it was originally and some pain may come and go. Complete healing may take up to a year or more.

MUSCLE OR TISSUE INJURY—COMMON WAYS OF TREATING:

- RICE method – Rest, Ice, Compression and Elevation. This is generally considered the first recommendation for treating a muscle or tendon injury and is the primary recommendation that a personal trainer should make. Wet cloth should be placed between ice or cold packs and the skin to avoid skin damage. Cold is applied for up to 20 minutes every 2 hours. Compression can be done by wrapping the area tightly without cutting off circulation. The injured area should be raised above the heart.
- Applying heat to an injury can make the area feel better, but too much heat is not good for swelling.
- Massage can help with blood circulation and loosening tense areas.
- Traction can be recommended by doctors or physical therapists and involves placing the joint in a position that may increase healing.

MUSCLE SORENESS—TWO TYPES:

1. **Acute muscle soreness** happens while the person is working and continues right after the activity is stopped. Lactate builds up within the muscle in the absence of oxygen, and the muscle may become temporarily inflamed. This pain should go away almost as soon as the activity is stopped.
2. **Delayed onset muscle soreness** (also called DOMS) happens 1-2 days after the workout. The reasons for this are not known, but theories include damage done to the muscles during the workout and swelling due to increased immune response.
   Activities that work the opposing muscle groups (eccentric actions) are more likely to cause DOMS. Many trainers recommend stretching or cooling the muscles after the workout, although this has not been proven to reduce DOMS.

Soreness can cause some clients to stop the program, while other clients feel that soreness is evidence of the work they did. Personal trainers should note the client's expectations.

COMMON INJURIES OF THE SHOULDER; WAYS TO PREVENT:

Rotator cuff tendinitis –

- strengthen the supraspinatus, subscapularis, infraspinatus, and teres minor
- remind people that as the arm raises in front of the body, the top of the shoulder should lower.
- If the arms are being raised over the shoulders, the arms should also move out to the sides a little bit
- Avoid the upright row, lat pulldowns with the bar behind the head, overhead presses with the bar behind the head, or any activity in which the arms are lifted over the shoulders in front of the body.

Impingement syndrome –

- avoid moving arms over the shoulder without moving arms out to the side a little.

***Biceps tendinitis* –**
- avoid lifting too-heavy weights or contracting muscles too fast.

***Shoulder dislocation or subluxation* –**
- avoid doing lat pulldowns with the bar behind the head, or other activities that move the arms out and to the side extensively.

COMMON INJURIES OF THE ELBOW AND WRIST; WAYS TO PREVENT:
Tennis elbow (lateral epicondylitis) and ***golfer's elbow*** (medial epicondylitis) –
- work the muscles in the forearm, including the wrist extensors, wrist flexors, wrist pronators, and wrist supinators
- Keep the wrist muscles flexible
- In any activity that is not designed to work the wrist, make sure the wrist is straight.
- Reduce the movement of the wrist in daily life.

Carpal tunnel syndrome (CTS) –
- keep the wrist from bending when doing daily activities or any exercises
- keep arms and wrists warm
- type with a gentle action
- give the wrists a rest frequently
- stretch wrist muscles

COMMON INJURIES TO THE HIP AND PELVIS; WAYS TO PREVENT:
- Iliotibial band tendinitis (ITB) involves the iliotibial band being too tight because of being overused. To avoid this, do not run downhill, and be sure to stretch the iliotibial band.
- Piriformis syndrome is damage to the hip external rotators, or the sciatic nerve getting pressure from the piriformis muscle. Stretching usually will prevent this and make it feel better.
- Adductor and hamstring strains happen often to those who work too hard without proper preparation. Warming up the muscles before activity can help, as well as stretching.
- Osteoarthritis may result in the disintegration of the connective tissues, and subsequent bone damage. Working the hip muscles gently can help improve the condition over time, although it is not preventable.

COMMON INJURIES TO THE KNEE:
- Patellofemoral pain syndrome is pain at the front of the knee caused by improper alignment of the kneecap so that it rubs against the femur.
- Patellar tendinitis is pain below the kneecap where it joins the lower leg, due to swelling of the patellar tendon.
- Iliotibial band syndrome involves the iliotibial band being too tight because of being overused.
- Ligament injuries are common in tendons around the knee, including the anterior cruciate ligament (ACL).
- Meniscus tears are caused by hitting the knee and damaging the cartilage or by overextending the knee. If a piece of meniscus breaks off and becomes stuck in the knee, it may prevent any movement and cause swelling and pain.
- Knee osteoarthritis involves the disintegration of the tissues cushioning the knee, resulting in pain.
- Knee bursitis involves the fluid pouches around the knee becoming swollen.

WAYS TO PREVENT KNEE INJURIES:

- Working the quadriceps and hamstrings and stretching the hamstrings, calves, and quadriceps.
- Increase strength in the vastus medialis.
- Work the knee by doing both activities that let the legs move freely (open kinetic chain) and activities that plant the feet (closed kinetic chain) and bend the knee.
- Do less bending of the knee, particularly in people who have had previous injuries or pain.
- To prevent iliotibial band syndrome, do not run downhill, and be sure to stretch the iliotibial band.
- For ACL injuries, the healing process is long, so once workouts are recommended by the physician, the trainer should focus on working the knee flexors and extensors.
- Focus on the correct way to bend the knee.

COMMON INJURIES OF THE LOWER LEG; WAYS TO PREVENT:

- Shin splints are pains in the lower leg that are caused by a variety of things, including tibial stress syndrome and fractures, periostitis, and anterior compartment syndrome. In general, activities in which the leg repeatedly receives an impact load will cause shin splints.
- Anterior compartment syndrome is a condition in which the leg muscles swell so much that the blood flow to the muscles is limited, which can damage the muscle.
- To avoid injury, try to run only on spongy or springy surfaces, wear shoes that cushion the foot, warm up before exercise and cool down at the end of workouts, keep the calves flexible and the dorsiflexors strong, and progress to higher weights slowly.

TWO COMMON INJURIES OF THE ANKLE AND FOOT; WAYS TO PREVENT:

1. **Achilles tendinitis** – Damage to the Achilles tendon or the surrounding areas. This can happen because of overworking the legs, misaligned legs, inadequate shoes, and quick movements of the tendon. It may lead to a rupture of the tendon.
   - To avoid this, stretch and work the gastrocnemius and the soleus, do not run uphill often, warm up the body before beginning an activity, wear appropriate shoes, and avoid overstretching the Achilles tendon.
2. **Ankle sprains** – Overstretching the connecting tissues around the ankle due to a shock to the area, usually when the sole of the foot turns inward (rolling the ankle to the side) and upward. This often results in repeated injuries.
   - To avoid this, work the tibialis anterior, extensor digitorum longus, peroneus tertius, the extensor digitorum longus, the peroneus brevis, peroneus tertius and peroneus longus, stretch the calf muscles, and wear ankle-supporting shoes if the area is damaged repeatedly.

ADDITIONAL COMMON INJURIES OF THE ANKLE AND FOOT; WAYS TO PREVENT:

1. **Plantar fasciitis** – Also called heel spur syndrome, is a swelling of the muscles and tissues running along the sole of the foot. This can lead to calcium deposits on the heels, and pain when first standing up in the morning.
   - To avoid this, wear appropriate shoes, with arch support and cushioned heels, put ice on the heel if pain is felt, reduce the number of exercises with weights, stretch and work the entire foot.
2. **Metatarsalgia** – Pain in the ball of the foot, often from jumping or bouncing or the arch of the foot falling.
   - To avoid this, wear appropriate shoes and do fewer jumping activities.

COMMON POSTURES OF THE UPPER BACK THAT INCREASE LIKELIHOOD OF INJURY; WAYS TO IMPROVE AND REDUCE INJURY:

1. The forward head position involves the head and upper back curving and dropping forward, leading to pain in the ligament that runs along the spine, tense and tired muscles around the spine, pain in the facet joints of the spine, pinched nerves and blood vessels in the upper back and neck, pain in the jaw or head, or having some muscles being too strong or tight and some being too weak.
   - To avoid this, keep the upper trapezius, levator scapulae, and scalenes flexible, point out the posture to the person, help the person feel the proper alignment, do not do extreme head tilting activities.
2. Excessive kyphosis involves a rounded back with the shoulder blades pulled apart.
   - To avoid this, work the middle trapezius, rhomboids, posterior deltoids, thoracic erector spinae, external rotator cuff muscles, and scapular depressors. Also stretch the pectoralis major, anterior deltoids, latissimus dorsi, and the internal shoulder rotators.

MAIN CAUSES OF LOW BACK PAIN:
   - Excessive lordosis is when the lower back is bent farther back than normal.
   - Tight hamstrings prevent people from lifting things with the proper posture.
   - Ruptured disk involves the tissues between vertebrae ripping and the bones pressing on the spinal nerve.
   - Sacroiliac pain happens when someone has one leg longer than another.
   - Spondylolysis is a tiny break in a part of the vertebra.
   - Spondylolisthesis involves a vertebra in the lower back slipping onto the vertebra right under it.
   - Cancer of the spine happens infrequently.
   - Ankylosing spondylitis is a condition in which the ligaments along the spine harden, and the vertebrae lose calcium.
   - Osteoarthritis may cause the disks between vertebrae to wither and let the bones get closer, and the facet joints may then begin to hold the weight of the body and thus develop bone spurs.
   - Scoliosis is a condition in which the spine curves to the side.

TYPE OF PROGRAM A TRAINER SHOULD RECOMMEND FOR A PERSON RECENTLY TREATED FOR LOW-BACK PAIN; MOVEMENTS TO BE AVOIDED IN ORDER TO PREVENT BACK INJURY:
   - ✓ Do many relaxation and stretching activities.
   - ✓ Focus on being aware of posture in daily life and in workouts. Drawing in and tightening the torso muscles should be practiced.
   - ✓ Focus on erector spinae stretches, quadratus lumborum stretches, iliopsoas stretches, hamstring stretches, and activities that move the back gently to increase flexibility.
   - ✓ Work on the weakest or too-long muscles.
   - ✓ Suggest the person lose weight and stop smoking.
   - ✓ Have the person avoid doing any bending of the back (either forward, backward or to the side) without supporting the upper body. When bending backwards, make sure the bend is small. When lifting an extremity (leg, arm, head), doing so without bending the limb may be more stressful on the back, so modify these with bent knees, arms, working one limb at a time, or doing a smaller lift.

STRENGTH AND SAFETY GUIDELINES

To develop strength with your clients and to help avoid injuries and soreness, follow these guidelines when setting up strength and fitness programs:

- Make sure that the client is fit for physical activities before you begin an exercise program. If an individual is not in good physical condition, he/she is more susceptible to injury.
- Make sure that the client warms up before beginning any type of activity. Begin with slow, easy exercises such as stretching and jumping jacks.
- Make sure that the client cools down after vigorous activities to avoid sore muscles.
- Make sure that the client is dressed properly for exercise. Clothes should fit loosely so that free movement is encouraged. The client should wear shoes designed to support and protect feet during exercise.
- Make sure that the exercise area is safe. Check for holes, objects, and uneven spots.
- Avoid using equipment that may cause injury.
- If you suspect an injury has occurred, stop immediately and seek medical attention.
- Also make sure that your client is re-hydrated before, during and after exercising.
- Do not have your client exercise immediately after meals – wait at least ½ hour.
- Postpone exercise at times of strong emotion, fatigue, or illness.

SETTING UP A PERSONAL TRAINING BUSINESS

WRITING A MISSION STATEMENT FOR YOUR PERSONAL TRAINING BUSINESS—THINGS TO CONSIDER:

A mission statement gives your customers an idea of what services you will provide, as well as your perspective on health and wellness. Before developing a mission statement for your customers to understand you, you should define for yourself what your mission will be.

1. Define for yourself what your purpose in life is.
2. Project a view of your future and determine what you would like to see for yourself.
3. Develop a statement that will define how you will accomplish your goals every day.
4. Define for yourself what you treasure in life.
5. Make promises to yourself as to what you will do in order to accomplish your goals.

WRITING A BUSINESS PLAN:

1. Determine what the needs are where you would like to work, and whether your personal and career goals match those needs. Your skills and preferences will influence the types of customers you will reach out for.
2. Your business plan should be written for the customer base you want to reach. Business plans must include your purpose and objectives, where, when and how you will operate, how you will fund the business, how you will advertise to prospective customers, whether or not you will hire other employees and how they will be paid and managed, what services you will offer, and what costs the business will incur.
3. Start your business, using your plan as a guide.
4. Assess at regular intervals how well the business is operating and determine whether you should make changes (such as reaching out to new customers, buying new equipment, pursuing more education, etc.).

POLICIES YOU SHOULD SET FOR YOUR BUSINESS:

- Determine your rates for personal fitness training, as well as additional services you may provide. Rates should be relative to the local trends and your experience and training.
- Develop policies about when fees are due, and have customers sign an agreement to that effect.
- Develop policies for customers who do not arrive on time or at all for a session. Many professionals charge for any session that was not cancelled prior to 24-hours before the session was scheduled.
- Develop standards for which customers you can work with, and which ones you must refuse. These standards will be based on answers to fitness assessments you perform on new customers, but may also depend on the behavior of the customer (those who frequently miss sessions, for instance, might be dropped from your business if you choose). These standards must be clearly laid out for customers, in writing, at the first session.

STRATEGIES FOR PROMOTING YOUR BUSINESS:

- ✓ Present yourself professionally, and focus on the type of customer you would like to work with.
- ✓ Find the customers you want where they will be. Develop other referral networks, including other health or fitness professionals or retail stores that sell health or fitness items.
- ✓ Offer yourself as a resource for speaking engagements.
- ✓ Write articles for local publications, or develop messages for television or radio.
- ✓ Send out a press release announcing your business to local publications.
- ✓ Offer incentives to customers who refer others to you.
- ✓ Provide a free consultation to new customers.
- ✓ Offer gift certificates for sale.
- ✓ Use direct mail, or hand out flyers.
- ✓ Develop a website.
- ✓ Volunteer with non-profit organizations to gain exposure.
- ✓ Work with another professional to offer services that would compliment yours.
- ✓ Contact manufacturers for possible sponsorships, and use current customers as references in advertising.
- ✓ Highlight any special skills (other languages spoken).
- ✓ Ask for help from experts.

WAYS YOU CAN REDUCE YOUR RISK OF LIABILITY:

- In delivering your services, you should adhere to the standard of care established by the national, professional organizations.
- Be sure to have customers sign an informed consent form that details their assumption of risk. This document should detail the possibility of injury when engaging in a fitness program, as well as the positive outcomes that can be expected.
- Customers may also be asked to sign a document that releases the trainer from liability in case of injury. Legal advice should be consulted in crafting these documents, as the language in such forms is crucial when determining the level of liability.
- Trainers should consider buying liability insurance, which will help protect personal assets in case of liability.
- Trainers should keep accurate records, stay current on education and certification, reevaluate customer programs frequently, and keep safety a priority in your practice.
- Develop a procedure to follow in an emergency.

TRAINER-CLIENT INTERACTION

BARRIERS TO ACTIVE LISTENING:
- ✓ Focusing on yourself and comparing yourself to others.
- ✓ Thinking about what you will say next.
- ✓ Selectively listening, losing focus, or ignoring some things being said.
- ✓ Passing judgments or criticizing the customer or others.
- ✓ Having to always be correct and not acknowledging your mistakes.
- ✓ Finding many ways in which the customer's situation is like yours may lead you to project your own perspectives into their speech.
- ✓ Trying to give advice too soon before you hear the whole picture.
- ✓ Switching to a different subject or dismissing what the customer is saying.
- ✓ Trying too hard to be liked, and only saying or doing what you think will make the person like you.
- ✓ Diminishing the seriousness of the customer's issues or denying their existence, which will then make your advice and service seem less important and make the person feel ignored.

HOW TO VERBALLY SUPPORT SOMEONE THROUGH ACTIVE LISTENING; OPEN-ENDED AND CLOSED-ENDED QUESTIONS:
- ✓ Repeat what the customer says, either exactly as spoken or in a different way, so that you can make sure you are hearing what she means to say.
- ✓ Request that the customer define more clearly what she is trying to say.
- ✓ Ask more open-ended questions to get more information.
- ✓ Recognize what the customer is saying and show that you understand.
- ✓ Review what the customer has said, then make sure the person agrees. Ask more questions if you do not understand something.

Open-ended questions cannot be answered with one word or by yes/no. Open-ended questions will require longer and more detailed answers and can give the interviewer more information. *Closed-ended questions* will be able to be answered with short, fact-based answers, including yes/no questions.

WEB LINKS INFO – Specific Exercise Review

For a specific exercise review, check out the links featured on the following page:

Use the link: http://www.mo-media.com/exercises
        http://www.mo-media.com/exercises

ONE REP MAX (1RM)

Here is an interesting chart, which should be able to help you in calculating projected 1 RM's. This will make it easier for you to decide how much weight your client should try, as it gives you a good ball park figure.

Relationships between reps and % maximum load for one rep maximum (1RM).

One Rep Max Calculations	
Repetitions	**Coefficient**
1	1
2	1.047
3	1.091
4	1.130
5	1.167
6	1.202
7	1.236
8	1.269
9	1.300
10	1.330
11	1.359
12	1.387
13	1.416
14	1.445
15	1.475
16	1.504
17	1.531
18	1.560
19	1.587
20	1.616

Here's a chart you can use to estimate one rep max for specific lifts.

Repetitions	Squat	Benchpress	Deadlift
1	1.0	1.0	1.0
2	1.0475	1.035	1.065
3	1.13	1.08	1.13
4	1.1575	1.115	1.147
5	1.2	1.15	1.164
6	1.242	1.18	1.181
7	1.284	1.22	1.198
8	1.326	1.255	1.232
9	1.368	1.29	1.232
10	1.41	1.325	1.24

Practice Test

Practice Questions

1. The joint movement that results in an increase of the joint angle is called
    a. Abduction
    b. Adduction
    c. Extension
    d. Flexion

2. Which of these muscles is not part of the Rotator cuff?
    a. Supraspinatus
    b. Infraspinatus
    c. Teres minor
    d. Teres major

3. Which of the following should be considered a life-threatening medical emergency?
    a. Anterior cruciate ligament tear
    b. A dislocation of the cervical spinal cord
    c. An Achilles' tendon rupture
    d. A hip fracture in an elderly individual

4. Which of the following can cause pain in the lumbar area?
    a. Strain of the tibialis anterior muscle
    b. Strain of the longissimus thoracis muscle
    c. Strain of the gastrocnemius muscle
    d. Strain of the sternocleidomastoid muscle

5. When working with a trainer, an individual lifts a 10-pound weight straight over her head through a distance of 2.5 feet. How much linear work has been generated?
    a. 4 pound-feet
    b. 7.5 pound-feet
    c. 25 pound-feet
    d. 50 pound-feet

6. For average groups of people represented below, which order represents the lowest resting heart rate to the highest resting heart rate?
    a. Men, women, children, elderly individuals
    b. Children, women, elderly individuals, men
    c. Elderly individuals, women, men, children
    d. Elderly individuals, men, women, children

7. The body recruits type I muscle fibers for activities of
    a. long duration and low intensity
    b. long duration and high intensity
    c. short duration and high intensity
    d. none of the above

8. All of the following classes of nutrients provide sources of energy EXCEPT
    a. proteins
    b. vitamins
    c. fats
    d. carbohydrates

9. A nonathlete who weighs 80 kg would require _____ grams per day of protein.
    a. 50 grams
    b. 80 grams
    c. 64 grams
    d. 100 grams

10. A deficiency of which vitamin can lead to difficulty seeing at night and an increased susceptibility to infections?
    a. vitamin B1
    b. vitamin B3
    c. vitamin E
    d. vitamin A

11. You are exercising outdoors and become concerned that your client may be dehydrated. At what point would her condition be considered a medical emergency?
    a. When she complains that her leg muscles are cramping
    b. When she seems to be confused and doesn't know where she is
    c. When she becomes dizzy and light-headed
    d. When she begins complaining of a headache

12. What food information is NOT present on a food label?
    a. amount of protein in a serving
    b. amount of cholesterol in a serving
    c. amount of calories in a serving
    d. amount of caffeine in a serving

13. When meeting with a client for the first time, all of the following can be helpful comments to make to a client EXCEPT
    a. "How would you like this work to help you?"
    b. "Can you tell me about your daily routine?"
    c. "What heath problems do you have?"
    d. "Do you think you have clinical depression?"

14. A client in the precontemplation stage of behavior might think to himself:
    a. "I just can't lose weight."
    b. "I have a plan to lose weight."
    c. "I am really thinking about how to lose weight."
    d. "I am so proud I lost weight!"

15. An example of a substitution behavioral change that you might suggest to a client is
    a. "Call your best friend to walk with you every day."
    b. "Take the stairs instead of the elevator at work."
    c. "If you reach this goal we set up, you can have a reward of your choosing."
    d. "Put your running shoes right by your bed so you are motivated to run first thing in the morning."

16. Your client is in the maintenance stage of behavior and is exercising regularly. One day she cancels her appointments with you, claiming she has too much to do at work. If she abandons her exercise routine completely, it is called a
    a. lapse
    b. self-change
    c. relapse
    d. self-challenge

17. All of the following can help the client-trainer relationship EXCEPT
    a. Accepting your client for what she is able to do, even if others her age are able to do more
    b. Asking your client about his week
    c. Answering a text or phone call during a session
    d. Keeping information between the two of you confidential

18. An example of active listening is
    a. "Why didn't you do this exercise this week?"
    b. "Great job with your exercises this week!"
    c. "How did your big project at work turn out?"
    d. "So you are saying that you didn't understand how this exercise was supposed to feel?"

19. The interactive tool that can lead to change by creating an equal partnership between the client and the trainer is called
    a. Motivational interviewing
    b. Generative moments
    c. Appreciative inquiry
    d. Change talk

20. Goals that a trainer helps a client set should be all of the following EXCEPT
    a. Time-limited
    b. Action-based
    c. Broadly defined
    d. Measurable

21. Active listening, building rapport, and showing understanding of a client's situation are all components of
    a. Nonverbal communication
    b. Intrinsic motivation
    c. Extrinsic motivation
    d. Client-centered techniques

22. As a prelude to creating a personal training package for a client, a trainer should obtain all of the following EXCEPT
    a. Approval and signature of a physician
    b. Informed consent from the client
    c. Permission to post the client's photo on the trainer's Web site
    d. Health history of the client

23. A number of atherosclerotic cardiovascular disease risk factors exist. A client who has which of the following would be considered to have a positive risk factor for hypertension?
    a. Systolic blood pressure $\geq$ 140 mm Hg on two separate occasions
    b. Diastolic blood pressure $\geq$75 mm Hg on two separate occasions
    c. Systolic blood pressure $\geq$ 140 mm Hg and diastolic blood pressure $\geq$ 100 mm Hg on one occasion
    d. Having taken an antihypertensive medication in the past

24. Shortness of breath at rest is called
    a. Ischemia
    b. Dyspnea
    c. Syncope
    d. Orthopnea

25. All of the following are true of intermittent claudication EXCEPT
    a. People with diabetes have a greater risk of having intermittent claudication.
    b. Intermittent claudication does not usually occur when a client stands or sits.
    c. Intermittent claudication usually goes away within 10 minutes of stopping an exercise.
    d. Symptoms associated with intermittent claudication are reproducible.

26. Which of the following pulses is not commonly used to determine an individual's heart rate?
    a. Carotid
    b. Brachial
    c. Radial
    d. Popliteal

27. Normal systolic and diastolic blood pressure measurements (in mm Hg) include which of the following?
    a. Systolic 110, diastolic 75
    b. Systolic 130, diastolic 70
    c. Systolic 140, diastolic 85
    d. Systolic 110, diastolic 85

28. An individual weighs 80 kg and is 3 meters tall. What range does his BMI fall into?
    a. Normal
    b. Overweight
    c. Obese class I
    d. Obese class II

29. The Rockport is a field test that involves
    a. Running continuously for 1.5 miles
    b. Walking intermittently for 2 miles
    c. Stepping up and down continuously for 3 minutes
    d. Walking as fast as possible for 1 mile

30. An individual's flexibility can be assessed by which of the following?
    a. A one-repetition bench press
    b. A sit-and-reach test
    c. A push-up test
    d. A curl-up test

31. The hip joint is what type of joint?
    a. Ball-and-socket joint
    b. Hinge joint
    c. Cartilaginous joint
    d. Pivot joint

32. The primary function of the respiratory system is
    a. Delivering nutrients to tissues in the body
    b. Regulating the body's pH level
    c. Facilitating the exchange of oxygen and carbon dioxide
    d. Maintaining fluid volume to prevent dehydration

33. The type of stretching that requires assistance from a personal trainer is called
    a. Active stretching
    b. Passive stretching
    c. Ballistic stretching
    d. Static stretching

34. All of the following are benefits of increased flexibility EXCEPT
    a. Improved circulation
    b. Increased range of motion
    c. Improved coordination
    d. Increased chance of muscle injury

35. The condition that involves rapid breakdown of muscle tissue due to too much exercise, which can potentially result in kidney failure, is called
    a. Myoglobinuria
    b. Rhabdomyolysis
    c. Dialysis
    d. Proteinuria

36. Benefits of nonlinear periodized training programs include all of the following EXCEPT
    a. Using a progressive increase in the workout intensity
    b. Allowing for variation in the workout intensity
    c. Having a "power" training day
    d. Training both power and strength of muscles within one week

37. What is the approximate target heart rate for a 50-year-old man in beats per minute (bpm)?
    a. 75 to 120
    b. 85 to 110
    c. 85 to 145
    d. 120 to 160

38. An effective cardiorespiratory training program session should include all of these basic components EXCEPT
    a. Power phase
    b. Cool-down phase
    c. Warm-up phase
    d. Endurance phase

39. The "talk test" refers to
    a. The practice of speaking with your client before a training session to check in with the client
    b. The practice of talking with your client during the cool-down phase to see how the session felt.
    c. The ability of an individual while exercising to talk or respond to a trainer's questions without gasping for breath.
    d. The comfort level of a client to let a trainer know when an exercise is too hard.

40. Individuals with osteoporosis
    a. Should not do flexibility training exercises
    b. Should avoid twisting or flexing of the spine
    c. Should not worry about proper breathing techniques
    d. Are not more likely to develop fractures

41. Which of the following inhibits a person's joint flexibility?
    a. Having cold muscles
    b. Being a woman
    c. Having more relaxed muscles
    d. Having a more physically active lifestyle

42. Older adults should engage in an aerobic exercise program that provides which of the following?
    a. 25 minutes, 3 days a week of mild intensity aerobic activity
    b. 30 minutes, 3 days a week of moderate intensity aerobic activity
    c. 20 minutes, 5 days a week of vigorous intensity aerobic activity
    d. 30 minutes, 5 days a week of moderate intensity aerobic activity

43. Which of the following conditions is an absolute contraindication for exercising during pregnancy?
    a. Poorly controlled seizure disorder
    b. Ruptured membranes
    c. Heavy smoker
    d. Poorly controlled hypertension

44. Common complications of diabetes include all of the following EXCEPT
    a. Kidney problems
    b. Vision problems
    c. Hearing problems
    d. Peripheral nerve problems

45. How much weight loss is appropriate for an obese individual with a BMI greater than 30?
    a. 1 kg a week
    b. 2 kg a week
    c. 3 kg a week
    d. 4 kg a week

46. Which of the following is not covered when obtaining informed consent from a client?
    a. Benefits that the client should expect to gain
    b. Risks and discomfort that may be associated with the training program
    c. Purpose of the training program
    d. How much the training program will cost

47. The end of a bone is called the
    a. Epiphysis
    b. Periosteum
    c. Endosteum
    d. Diaphysis

48. All are true of a synovial joint EXCEPT
    a. The synovial cavity is filled with synovial fluid.
    b. A synovial joint can flex and extend.
    c. A synovial joint may be supported by ligaments.
    d. A synovial joint never contains any other structures inside of it.

49. Leg raises are an example of
    a. Hip extension
    b. Knee flexion
    c. Hip flexion
    d. Hip abduction

50. Which function does the autonomic nervous system NOT regulate?
    a. Digestion
    b. Breathing
    c. Running
    d. Secretion of hormones

Answer Key and Explanations

1. C: When a joint is extended, the angle of the joint is increased. Flexion is the opposite of extension, and causes the joint angle to decrease. Abduction refers to movement that is directed away from the midline of the body. The opposite of abduction is adduction. Adduction describes movements that are made toward the midline of the body.

2. D: The Supraspinatus is an abductor of the arm. The Infraspinatus and Teres minor are both external rotators. The Subscapularis is the missing muscle of the rotator cuff.

3. B: Any trauma to the neck (or cervical spine) should be considered a medical emergency. When the cervical vertebrae are dislocated or fractured, the spinal column can become unstable. This can potentially lead to paralysis or death. While an Achilles' tendon rupture or anterior cruciate ligament tear is a serious leg/knee injury, respectively, and may be career ending for athletes, either one is not life threatening. A hip fracture or a fracture of the neck of the femur can cause permanent disability, especially in the elderly. However, these are also not usually life threatening.

4. B: The longissimus thoracis muscle is located in the posterior lumbar region. It is part of the erector spinae group. These muscles help maintain posture and provide stability to the spine. Lumbar pain, also called low back pain, is one of the most common causes of disability. About 60 to 80% of the general population will experience it at some point in their lives. Determining the specific cause of lumbar pain may be difficult, but muscle strain, an intervertebral herniated disc, and joint inflammation can all cause lumbar pain. The other muscles are not located in the lumbar region. The sternocleidomastoid muscle is located in the cervical region. Strain to this muscle occurs with "whiplash" injuries. The tibialis anterior muscle is located on the anterior and lateral part of the lower leg. The gastrocnemius muscle is located on the posterior part of the lower leg.

5. C: Multiplying the force times the distance through which the force travels will result in the linear work generated. Ten times 2.5 equals 25.

6. D: Heart rate is the number of times that the heart beats per minute and can be measured by taking a pulse. Average people have a resting heart rate of 60 to 80 beats per minute (bpm). The elderly have a lower resting heart rate than adult men and women. Men have a resting heart rate that is about 10 bpm lower than that of adult women. Children have resting heart rates that are higher than those of adults. When comparing fit to unfit individuals, fit individuals have a lower resting heart rate.

7. A: The body has two types of muscle fibers: type I and type II. Together, these muscle fibers can do all types of tasks. However, the body recruits each type during different activities or specific times of an activity, depending on the type and duration of motion required. Type I muscle fibers, also called slow-twitch fibers, are used for activities of long duration and low intensity, such as those involving endurance. In contrast, type II muscle fibers are employed for high-speed, high-power tasks. These muscle fibers are capable of generating force more quickly than type I muscle fibers.

8. B: Carbon is critical for the energy production process. Proteins, fats, and carbohydrates—which are all sources of carbon—contribute to a number of functions in the body. They help provide energy so that muscles, nerves, and metabolic processes work normally. Energy is measured in calories (cal) or kilocalories (kcal). When individuals exercise, they can "burn" energy more quickly. Vitamins and minerals are critical for providing essential nutrients that the body needs to maintain normal function; however, they are not a source of energy.

9. C: The average person's daily requirement for protein is 0.8 g/kg. In other words, multiplying 0.8 by the person's weight in kilograms will give the daily amount of protein in grams needed. For this individual, that would be $80 \times 0.8 = 64$ grams. Athletes require more protein each day—about 1.2 to 2 g/kg of body weight. If this individual were an athlete, he or she would require between 96 and 160 grams of protein per day. In addition to these specific recommendations, it is also recommended that protein account for about 12 to 15% of the total calories a person eats each day.

10. D: Vitamin A, known as retinol, is found in foods such as fish liver oils, butter, and egg yolks. It is critical for red blood cell and embryo development and normal functioning of the eyes, the immune system, and the skin. Vitamin B_1 is also called thiamin. A deficiency of this vitamin can lead to beriberi. Symptoms of beriberi can include cardiovascular problems, peripheral neuropathy, and cognitive and psychiatric problems. Vitamin B_3 is also known as niacin; a deficiency of this vitamin can cause a disease called pellagra. Pellagra can cause a skin rash, gastrointestinal symptoms, or cognitive difficulties. If untreated, it can also lead to death. Vitamin E is an antioxidant that augments the immune system. It can help prevent cell membranes from being destroyed by harmful free radicals.

11. B: Dehydration, heat exhaustion, and heat stroke are conditions that are best avoided by encouraging clients to drink either water or sports drinks often. When individuals wait until they feel thirsty to drink, they may already have lost 1 to 2 liters of fluid. A dehydrated individual may feel less energetic and begin to develop muscle cramps. If not treated, an individual can develop heat exhaustion, which may be manifested by headaches and feelings of nausea. If heat exhaustion isn't treated, an individual may suffer from heat stroke. During heat stroke, an individual's body temperature increases, and he or she may become confused or lose consciousness. This is a medical emergency. The patient needs to have her body temperature lowered as quickly as possible.

12. D: Labeling on food packages is helpful in determining a number of characteristics of a food, including the ingredients, serving size, and nutrients present in the food. Food label information is based on a 2,000 calorie diet. It provides the percent daily value for the amount of fats, cholesterol, sodium, potassium, carbohydrates, and protein present in a serving size. While caffeine will be listed as an ingredient if it is present in the food, the specific amount of caffeine will not be listed.

13. D: It is important to remember that coaching is not therapy or mental health counseling. Personal trainers should never diagnose current psychiatric problems. However, it is important to ask a person about their past history—medical and otherwise—so that your sessions can be appropriate and productive. Knowing about a person's daily routine will tell you how active he or she usually is. Asking, "How would you like this work to help you?" can elicit a specific goal that the two of you can work toward.

14. A: There are five stages of behavioral change. Listed in order of unwilling to change to readiness to change, they are precontemplation, contemplation, preparation, action, and maintenance. People in precontemplation often say, "I can't" or "I won't" about being able to change. People in the contemplation stage often say, "I just may change" or "I'm thinking about it." People in the preparation stage have actively decided to take action at some point soon. In the action stage, a person has decided to implement a consistent change, but has been implementing the new behavior for less than six months. If a person has consistently implemented a change for more than six months, he or she is in the maintenance stage.

15. B: There are a number of strategies trainers can employ in order to effect behavior change in a client. Substitution or counterconditioning involves substituting healthy behaviors for unhealthy behaviors. Answer A is an example of social support. Answer C is an example of a reward or reinforcement system. Answer D is an example of environmental control, which is a cue that can precipitate healthy behavior.

16. C: A relapse is when a person stops their positive behavior and, as a result, loses the positive benefits he or she had gained. Many conditions can lead to relapse; work pressures, boredom, and increased travel are only a few. Although similar, a lapse is a temporary stop in positive behavior. Had this client returned after a week or two, her exercise routine would have lapsed, but she would have likely maintained or quickly regained the positive benefits.

17. C: A number of factors can help facilitate a beneficial working relationship between a client and a trainer. These can include being present in the moment, maintaining confidentiality, being interested in your client's life, giving helpful feedback, and treating your client in a positive way. Along those lines, it is important to accept clients at the level they are currently at, rather than comparing them to others.

18. D: Active listening is a technique than enhances communication. It involves conveying what the client says back to the client, so that the individual feels they are being heard and understood. The client tells you how he or she feels or what he or she thinks, and you repeat or paraphrase it back to the individual. This technique provides the opportunity for clarification in the event that the client actually meant something else. When actively listening, it is helpful to let the other speak without interruption and to maintain eye contact and focus on the client.

19. A: Motivational interviewing is based on the idea that change occurs when there is an equal partnership between the client and trainer. While you are a training expert, your client is an expert is his or her own life. Motivational interviewing is used in a client-centered relationship. Generative moments are powerful or negative events that have happened to a client that can spur him or her to change. Appreciative inquiry is a technique in which the trainer asks positive and powerful questions to help the client visualize potential possibilities. Change talk involves language spoken by a client about his or her desire and ability to change their behavior.

20. C: Goals that are most helpful are those that are specific, very well defined, able to be measured, realistic, and have a time constraint on them. The actions a client needs to take should be specifically defined. For example, a goal may be that a client will walk on his treadmill at a pace of 3 mph for 30 minutes on Monday through Friday before going to work.

21. D: Client-centered techniques include asking open-ended questions, listening actively, and frequently clarifying what the client says. These can all contribute to building rapport and a strong relationship with a client. Nonverbal communication is that which is expressed and

- 142 -

received via nonverbal cues, such as facial expressions, gestures, and the presence or absence of eye contact. Intrinsic motivation is the motivation for change that comes from within. For example, a person may want to lose weight to feel proud or to feel like he can achieve a goal. When people are extrinsically motivated, they are motivated to achieve a goal because of an external factor. For example, someone might want to lose weight to fit into a wedding dress.

22. C: While you should always obtain permission before posting a photo of a client on a Web site, that is not one of the critical initial pieces of information. If medical clearance is necessary, a signature and recommendations from your client's physician should be obtained. In addition, you will need to know your client's past and present medical and health issues to create an appropriate training plan. You will also need informed consent from your client, demonstrating that he or she understands the risk and benefits of undertaking a training program.

23. A: Hypertension is defined by the Seventh Report of the Joint National Committee on Prevention, Detection, Evaluation, and Treatment of High Blood Pressure as a systolic blood pressure of $\geq$ 140 mm Hg and a diastolic blood pressure of $\geq$ 90 mm Hg on two separate occasions. In addition, current use of an antihypertensive medication is considered to be a positive risk factor for hypertension.

24. B: A client with dyspnea will have shortness of breath while resting or only with mild exertion. It is not normal, and it can be a symptom of cardiac or pulmonary disease. Orthopnea is shortness of breath that occurs when one is lying down. It is relieved by sitting upright or standing. Ischemia occurs when there is a lack of blood flow and oxygen to the heart. This causes pain in the chest or pain that has radiated to the neck or arm. Syncope is a loss of consciousness that usually occurs when the brain does not receive enough oxygen.

25. C: When an individual has intermittent claudication, he or she will develop pain in a specific area with exercise due to inadequate blood flow to that specific muscle. This pain can be reproduced from day to day. It usually does not occur when a client is sitting or standing. People with coronary artery disease or diabetes are prone to developing intermittent claudication. However, once the exercise that precipitated the pain has stopped, the pain should go away within one to two minutes.

26. D: The popliteal artery, located behind the knee, can be difficult to palpate. The carotid pulse is felt by placing one's fingers lightly in the lower neck, along the medial aspect of the sternocleidomastoid muscle. The brachial pulse can be palpated between the triceps and biceps muscles on the anterior and medial aspect of the arm, near the elbow. The radial artery can be palpated on the anterior arm, near the wrist.

27. A: Normal blood pressure is classified as a systolic pressure of less than 120 mm Hg and a diastolic pressure of less than 80 mm Hg. If either the systolic or diastolic pressures are elevated on multiple occasions, an individual's blood pressure is considered to be high.

28. B: BMI stands for body mass index, and it can be calculated by dividing an individual's weight by height. In this example, BMI = 80 kg / 3 m. This results in a BMI of 26.7. BMI values fall into a range. The normal range is 18.5–24.9. The overweight range is 25–29.9. The obese class I range is 30–34.9. The obese class II range is 35–39.9.

29. D: The Rockport 1-mile walk test involves having a client walk as fast as he or she can for a distance of 1 mile. The individual must not run at all during this test. At the end of the test, the

individual's pulse and heart rate are measured. The Queens College Step Test involves having an individual step up and down on a standardized step height continuously for 3 minutes and then measuring his or her pulse and heart rate after the 3 minutes.

30. B: A sit-and-reach test can measure the flexibility of an individual's lower back, hip, and hamstrings. A one-repetition bench press is used to assess muscular strength or muscle force. Both the push-up test and the curl-up test are used for measuring muscle endurance.

31. A: The hip joint as well as the shoulder joint can move in all directions. They are ball-and-socket joints. A hinge joint can only move in one plane, such as with knee flexion and extension. A cartilaginous joint is a strong joint that is very slightly movable, such as intervertebral joints. A pivot joint is a joint in one plane that permits rotation, such as the humeroradial joint.

32. C: The respiratory system involves the lungs and is where the exchange of oxygen for carbon dioxide occurs. The cardiovascular system, which involves the heart and blood vessels, is responsible for delivering oxygen and nutrients to all tissues in the body, regulating the body's pH level to prevent acidosis or alkalosis, and maintaining fluid volume to prevent dehydration.

33. B: In passive stretching, a client remains relaxed, allowing a trainer to stretch the client's muscles. Ballistic stretching, which involves a bouncing-like movement, can cause injury to muscles if not performed carefully. Static stretching involves movements that are deliberate and sustained. Active stretching involves stretching muscles throughout their range of motion.

34. D: Flexibility training has a number of benefits, including increased circulation, increased range of motion, improved muscle coordination, and decreased future chance of muscle injury.

35. B: Rhabdomyolysis, caused when an individual exercises too excessively, results in muscle damage and breakdown. These breakdown products, which can include protein and myoglobin, then enter the bloodstream and have the potential to harm the kidneys. Kidney failure, and possibly death, can result. Symptoms of rhabdomyolysis can include muscle swelling, pain, and soreness. Myoglobinuria and proteinuria describe the conditions of having myoglobin and protein in the urine. However, they do necessarily reflect a cause. Dialysis is a treatment for kidney failure.

36. A: While a linear periodized training program involves having a progressive increase in the workout intensity over the course of a week, a nonlinear periodized training program involves variation of intensity over the course of a week. A weeklong nonlinear periodized training program can target both muscle strength and power. A "power" training day involving power sets can also be implemented. This type of program may be more conducive to individuals with scheduling conflicts.

37. C: To calculate an individual's target heart rate, first one needs to estimate the person's maximal heart rate. This is estimated by subtracting a person's age from 220. In this example, the person's maximal heart rate is 220 – 50 = 170. Using this number, the target heart rate can be calculated. The recommended target heart rate is between 50% and 85% of the maximal heart rate. This would be 170 × 0.50 = 85, and 170 × 0.85 = 145. So, the individual's target heart rate is estimated to be between about 85 and 145 bpm.

38. A: A training program needs to balance many different variables in order to be effective. A trainer needs to take a client's goals, daily routines, and preferences into account to create a

routine that will be followed. Each training session should include a warm-up phase, a workout or endurance phase, and then a cool-down phase.

39. C: It is important that a training session not be too intense. The "talk test" is a simple way to get a handle on the intensity of the endurance or workout phase. A client should be able to talk or answer a trainer's questions without gasping for breath. Not being able to speak easily can indicate that the workout is too intense. Cardiovascular, muscular, and orthopedic injuries are more likely to occur when a workout is too intense.

40. B: Osteoporosis is a disease that involves a loss of bone mineral density. Osteopenia is a milder form of osteoporosis. Although people with osteoporosis are more susceptible to fractures due to the thinning of their bones, they are appropriate candidates for flexibility training programs. These programs can help improve posture and maintain the alignment of the spine. However, the program should avoid repetitive exercises that involve twisting or flexing of the spine. Everyone who participates in a flexibility training program should be taught proper breathing techniques.

41. A: A person's flexibility is reflected in his or her ability to move a joint, without pain, through a range of motion. In general, a number of factors are associated with increased flexibility. Younger people are more flexible than older individuals, and women are more flexible than men. Warmer, more relaxed muscles allow more joint flexibility than colder muscles. Individuals who are physically active are often more flexible than those who are not. In addition, the joint structure and health of the joint and its surrounding tissues affect an individual's flexibility.

42. D: If their medical issues allow it, individuals over the age of 65 can and should participate in exercise training programs. Aerobic, or cardiorespiratory, exercise can decrease morbidity and mortality rates in older individuals. The recommendations are for older individuals to engage in moderate intensity aerobic activity for 30 minutes, 5 days a week (150 minutes total), or to engage in vigorous intensity aerobic activity for 25 minutes, 3 days a week (75 minutes total). People can also do a combination of both.

43. B: Recent research supports a role for exercise programs during pregnancy. Goals of this type of program can include reducing low back pain and decreasing the risk for developing gestational diabetes. However, there do exist a number of absolute contraindications. Some of these include ruptured membranes, placenta previa after 26 weeks of gestation, premature labor, preeclampsia, and high-risk multiple gestation pregnancies. In contrast, relative contraindications include the individual being a heavy smoker, having poorly controlled diabetes or seizures, or having poorly controlled hypertension or hyperthyroid disease.

44. C: Diabetes can lead to kidney problems (nephropathy), trouble seeing (retinopathy), and decreased sensation of peripheral nerves (peripheral neuropathy). If these conditions are present, a trainer needs to adapt an exercise program accordingly. Some precautions that can be taken include keeping the blood pressure stable for retinopathy, avoiding exercise requiring high levels of coordination for peripheral neuropathy, or avoiding prolonged exercise for nephropathy.

45. A: People who are obese have a BMI greater than or equal to 30. These individuals are at a high risk of cardiac problems, certain types of cancers, and diabetes. Among other areas, training programs can focus on weight loss, promoting appetite control, and lowering the risk of

associated medical issues. Weight loss should be gradual—not more than 1 kg per week. Aerobic training sessions five to seven times a week lasting 45–60 minutes per session may be helpful.

46. D: Obtaining informed consent at the beginning of a professional relationship can protect against potential later legal action. An informed consent document will discuss the reason for the training program, the risks or discomfort that a client may experience, the responsibilities of the client, the benefits the client may reap, and it will offer the opportunity for a client to ask related questions. Fee structure and payments are not part of the informed consent.

47. A: When describing the anatomy of a bone, the epiphysis is the end of a bone and the diaphysis is the shaft of the bone. The periosteum is a membrane that covers the surface of a bone, except at the articular surfaces (joints). The endosteum is the lining of the bone marrow cavity and contains the cells necessary for new bone development.

48. D: A synovial joint is the most common type of joint found in the body and is made up of two articulating bones. Synovial fluid is present in the synovial cavity, which is lined by a synovial membrane. The joint is surrounded by a fibrous capsule, which can be supported by ligaments. Sometimes, a synovial joint may contain other structures, such as menisci (for example, in the knee) or fat pads. There are subtypes of synovial joints, including a hinge joint, ball-and-socket joint, and a pivot joint.

49. C: Leg raises are one type of exercise that works the hip flexor muscles. These muscles include the iliopsoas, rectus femoris, sartorius, and pectineus. Exercises for hip extension include squats or leg presses. Hip extensor muscles are the hamstrings and the gluteus maximus. Hip abduction exercises can be done with an exercise machine. Muscles involved with hip abduction include the tensor fascia latae, sartorius, and gluteus minimus and medius. Leg curl exercises involve knee flexion. Muscles involved with flexion of the knee are the hamstrings, gracilis, and popliteus.

50. C: The central nervous system is comprised of the brain and the spinal cord and is responsible for receiving, analyzing, interpreting, and acting on sensory information. The central nervous system is comprised of the peripheral and autonomic nervous systems. The autonomic nervous system is responsible for functions such as respiration, digestion, making hormones, and maintaining heart rate. The autonomic nervous system can be subdivided into the sympathetic nervous system, which is activated when the body is "stressed" and causes an increase in heart rate and respiratory rate and the parasympathetic nervous system, which is "in control" when the stressful stimulus is no longer present.

Special Report: Which Study Guides and Practice Tests Are Worth Your Time?

We believe the following practice tests and guide present uncommon value to our customers who wish to "really study" for the NSCA-CPT test. While our manual teaches some valuable tricks and tips that no one else covers, learning the basic coursework tested on the exam is also necessary.

Practice Tests

Official Practice Test Questions
http://www.nsca-cc.org/exam_info/sample_exam.html

Study Guides

Materials offered by the NSCA
https://secure2.digitalims.net/nsca-cc.org/order/category.html?steps=cl&prod_category=NSCA-CPT+Examination+Review+Materials

These guides are THE best comprehensive coursework guides to the licensure exams. If you want to spend a couple months in preparation to squeeze every last drop out of your score, buy these books and videos!

Musculature/Innervation Review – Arm and Back

Muscle	Origin	Insertion	Nerve
Trapezius	Ext. Occipit Protuberance, Spines of T Vertebrae	Lateral Clavicle, Spine of the Scapula	Spinal Accessory Nerve CN XI
Latissimus Dorsi	Spines of Lower 6 T Vertebrae, Iliac Crest and Lower 4 Ribs	Bicipital Groove	Thoracodorsal
Levator Scapulae	Transverse Process of C1-C4	Upper Medial Border of Scapula	Dorsal Scapula
Rhomboid Major	Spinous Process of T2-T5	Medial Border Scapula Below Spine	Dorsal Scapular
Rhomboid Minor	Spinous Process of C7-T1	Medial Border Scapula Opp. Spine	Dorsal Scapular
Teres Major	Lateral Dorsal Inferior Angle of Scapula	Bicipital Groove	Lower Subscapular
Teres Minor	Lateral Scapula 2/3 way down	Greater Tubercle of Humerus	Axillary
Deltoid	Lateral 1/3 Clavicle & Acromion Process, Spine of the Scapula	Deltoid Tuberosity	Axillary
Supraspinatus	Supraspinatus Fossa	Greater Tubercle of Humerus	Suprascapular
Infraspinatus	Infaspinatus Fossa	Greater Tubercle of Humerus	Suprascapular
Subscapularis	Subscapular Fossa	Lesser Tubercle of Humerus	Upper and lower Subscapular
Serratus Anterior	Slips of Upper 8-9 Ribs	Ventral-Medial Border Scapula	Long Thoracic
Subclavius	Inferior Surface of the Clavicle	First Rib	Nerve to the Subclavius
Pectoralis Major	Medial ½ clavicle and Side of Sternum	Bicipital Groove	Medial and Lateral Pectoral
Pectoralis Minor	Ribs 3,4,5 or 2,3,4	Coracoid Process	Medial Pectoral
Biceps Branchii	Supraglenoid Tubercle	Posterior Margin of Radial Tuberosity	Musculocutaneous
Coracobrachialis	Coracoid Process	Medial Humerus at Deltoid Tuberosity Level	Musculocutaneous
Brachialis	Anterior-Lateral ½ of Humerus	Ulnar Tuberosity and Coronoid Process	Musculocutaneous
Triceps Brachii	Infraglenoid Tubercle, Below and Medial to the Radial Groove	Olecranon Process	Radial
Anconeus	Posterior, Lateral Humeral Condyle	Upper Posterior Ulna	Radial
Brachioradialis	Lateral Supracondylar Ridge of Humerus	Radial Styloid Process	Radial
Pronator Teres	Medial Epicondyle and Supracondylar Ridge	½ Way Down on Lateral Radius	Median
Pronator Quadratus	Distal-Medial Ulna	Distal-Lateral Radius	Anterior Interosseous

Musculature/Innervation Review – The Forearm

Muscle	Origin	Insertion	Nerve
Brachioradialis	Lateral Supracondylar Ridge of Humerus	Radial Styloid Process	Radial
Pronator Teres	Medial Epicondyle and Supracondylar Ridge	½ Way Down on Lateral Radius	Median
Pronator Quadratus	Distal-Medial Ulna	Distal-Lateral Radius	Anterior Interosseous
Supinator	Lateral Epicondyle of Humerus	Upper ½ Lateral, Posterior Radius	Posterior Inter-Deep Radial
Flexor Carpi Radialis	Medial Epicondyle of Humerus	2nd and 3rd Metacarpal	Median
Flexor Carpi Ulnaris	Medial Epicondyle of Humerus	Pisiform, Hamate, 5th Metacarpal	Ulnar
Palmaris Longus	Medial Epicondyle of the Humerus	Palmar Aponeurosis and Flexor Retinaculum	Median
Flexor Digitorum Suerficialis	Medial Epicondyle, Radius, Ulna	Medial 4 Digits	Median
Flexor Digitorum Profundus	Ulna, Interosseous Membrane	Medial 4 Digits (distal part)	Median (lateral 2 digits), Ulnar (median 2 digits)
Flexor Pollicis Longus	Radius	Distal Phalanx (thumb)	Anterior Inter-Deep Median
Extensor Carpi Radialis Longus	Lateral Condyle and Supracondylar Ridge	2nd Metacarpal	Radial
Extensor Carpi Radialis Brevis	Lateral Epicondyle of Humerus	3rd Metacarpal	Posterior Inter-Deep Radial
Extensor Carpi Ulnaris	Lateral Epicondyle of Humerus	5th Metacarpal	Posterior Inter-Deep Radial
Extensor Digitorum	Lateral Epicondyle of Humerus	Extension Expansion Hood of Medial 4 Digits	Posterior Inter-Deep Radial
Extensor Digiti Minimi	Lateral Epicondyle of Humerus	Extension Expansion Hood of (little finger)	Posterior Inter-Deep Radial
Abductor Pollicis Longus	Posterior Radius and Ulna	Radial Side of 1st Metacarpal	Posterior Inter-Deep Radial
Extensor Indicis	Ulna and Interosseous Membrane	Extension Expansion Hood (index finger)	Posterior Inter-Deep Radial
Extensor Pollicis Longus	Ulna and Interosseous Membrane	Distal Phalanx (thumb)	Posterior Inter-Deep Radial
Extensor Pollicis Brevis	Radius	Proximal Phalanx (thumb)	Posterior Inter-Deep Radial

Musculature/Innervation Review – The Hand

Muscle	Origin	Insertion	Nerve
Adductor Policis	Capitate and Base of Adjacent Metacarpals	Proximal Phalanx (thumb)	Deep Branch of Ulnar
Lumbricals	Tendons of Flexor Digitorum Profundas	Extension Expansion Hood of Medial 4 Digits	Deep Branch Ulnar (medial 2 Ls), Median (lateral 2 Ls)
Dorsal Interosseous Muscles (4)	Sides of Metacarpals	Extension Expansion Hood of Digits 2-4	Deep Branch Ulnar
Palmar Interosseous (3)	Sides of Metacarpals	Extension Expansion Hood, Digits 2,4,5	Deep Branch Ulnar
Palmaris Brevis	Anterior Flexor Retinaculum and Palmar Aponeurosis	Skin-Ulnar Border of Hand	Superficial Ulnar
Abductor Pollicis Brevis	Flexor Retinaculum, Trapezium	Lateral Proximal Phalanx (thumb)	Median (thenar branch)
Flexor Pollicis Brevis	Flexor Retinaculum, Trapezium	Lateral Proximal Phalanx (thumb)	Median (thenar branch)
Opponens Pollicis	Flexor Retinaculum, Trapezium	Radial Border (1st Metacarpal)	Median (thenar branch)
Abductor Digiti Minimi	Flexor Retinaculum, Pisiform	Proximal Phalanx (little finger)	Deep Branch Ulnar
Flexor Digiti Minimi	Flexor Retinaculum, Hamate	Proximal Phalanx (little finger)	Deep Branch Ulnar
Opponens Digiti Minimi	Flexor Retinaculum, Hamate	Ulnar Medial Border (5th Metacarpal)	Deep Branch Ulnar

Musculature/Innervation Review – The Thigh

Muscle	Origin	Insertion	Nerve
Psoas Major	Bodies and Discs of T12-L5	Lesser Trochanter	L2,3
Psoas Minor	Bodies and Discs of T12 and L1	Pectineal Line of Superior Pubic Bone	L2,3
Iliacus	Upper 2/3 Iliac Fossa	Lesser Trochanter	Femoral L2-4
Pectinius	Pubic Ramus	Spiral Line	Femoral
Iliposoas	Joining of Psoas Major and Iliacus	Lesser Trochanter	L2-4
Piriformis	Anterior Surface of the Sacrum	Greater Trochanter	S1, S2
Obturator Internus	Inner Surface of the Obturator Membrane	Greater Trochanter	Sacral Plexus
Obturator Externus	Outer Surface of the Obturator Membrane	Greater Trochanter	Obturator
Gemellus Superior	Ischial Spine	Greater Trochanter	Sacral Plexus
Gemellus Inferior	Ischial Tuberosity	Greater Trochanter	Sacral Plexus
Quadratus Femoris	Ischial Tuberosity	Quadrate Tubercle of the Femur	Sacral Plexus
Gluteus Maximus	Outer Surface of Ilium, Sacrum and Coccyx	Iliotibial Tract, Gluteal Tubercle of the Femur	Inferior Gluteal
Gluteus Minimus	Outer Surface of the Ilium	Greater Trochanter	Superior Gluteal
Gluteus Medius	Outer Surface of the Ilium	Greater Trochanter	Superior Gluteal
Satorius	Anterior Superior Iliac Spine	Upper Medial Tibia	Femoral
Quadriceps Femoris	Anterior Inferior Iliac Spine, Femur-Lateral and Medial	Tibial Tuberosity	Femoral
Gracilis	Pubic Bone	Upper Medial Tibia	Obturator (anterior branch)
Abductor Longus	Pubic Bone	Linea Aspera	Obturator (anterior branch)
Abductor Brevis	Pubic Bone	Linea Aspera	Obturator (anterior branch)
Abductor Magnus	Pubic Bone	Entire Linea Aspera	Sciatic, Obturator
Tensor Faciae Latae	Iliac Crest	Iliotibial Band	Superior Gluteal
Biceps Femoris	Ischial Tuberosity, Linea Aspera	Head of Fibula, Lateral Condyle of Tibia	Sciatic-Tibial portion and Common Peroneal Portion
Semimembranosus	Ischial Tuberosity	Upper Medial Tibia	Sciatic-Tibial Portion
Semitendinosus	Ischial Tuberosity	Upper Medial Tibia	Sciatic-Tibial Portion

Musculature/Innervation Review – The Calf and Foot

Muscle	Origin	Insertion	Nerve
Tibialis Anterior	Upper 2/3 Lateral Tibia and Interosseous Membrane	1st Cuneiform and Base of 1st Metatarsal	Deep Peroneal
Extensor Digitorum Longus	Upper 2/3 Fibula and Interosseous Membrane	4 Tendons-Distal Middle Phalanges	Deep Peroneal
Extensor Hallucis Longus	Middle 1/3 of Anterior Fibula	Base of Distal Phalanx of Big Toe	Deep Peroneal
Peroneus Tertius	Distal Fibula	Base of 5th Metatarsal	Deep Peroneal
Extensor Hallucis Brevis	Dorsal Calcaneus	Extensor Digitorum Longus Tendons	Deep Peroneal
Peroneus Longus	Upper 2/3 Lateral Fibula	1st Metatarsal and 1st Cuneiform	Superficial Peroneal
Peroneus Brevis	Lateral Distal Fibula	5th Metatarsal Tuberosity	Superficial Peroneal
Soleus	Upper Shaft of Fibula	Calcaneus via Achilles Tendon	Tibial
Flexor Digitorum Longus	Middle 1/3 of Posterior Tibia	Base of Distal Phalanx of Lateral 4 Toes	Tibial
Flexor Hallucis Longus	Middle and Lower 1/3 of Posterior Tibia	Distal Phalanx of Big Toe	Tibial
Tibialis Posterior	Posterior Upper Tibia, Fibula	Navicular Bone and 1st Cuneiform	Tibial
Popliteus	Upper Posterior Tibia	Lateral Condyle of Femur	Tibial
Flexor Digitorum Brevis	Calcaneus	Middle Phalanges of Lateral 4 Toes	Medial Plantar
Abductor Hallucis	Calcaneus	Medial Proximal Phalanx of Big Toe	Medial Plantar
Abductor Digiti Brevis	Calcaneus	Lateral Proximal Phalanx of Big Toe	Lateral Plantar
Quadratus Plantae	Lateral and Medial Side of the Calcaneus	Tendons of Flexor Digitorum Longus	Lateral Plantar
Lumbricals	Tendons of Flexor Digitorum Longus	Extensor Tendons of Toes	Medial Plantar/ Lateral Plantar
Flexor Hallucis Brevis	Cuboid Bone	Splits on Base of Proximal Phalanx of Big Toe	Medial Plantar
Flexor Digiti Minimi Brevis	Base of 5th Metatarsal	Base of Proximal Phalanx of Little Toe	Lateral Plantar
Abductor Hallucis	Metatarsals 2-4	Base of Proximal Phalanx of Big Toe	Lateral Plantar
Interossei	Sides of Metatarsal Bones	Base of 1st Phalanx and Extensor Tendons	Lateral Plantar

CPR REVIEW / CHEAT SHEET

Topic	New Guidelines
Conscious Choking	5 back blows, then 5 abdominal thrusts- adult/child
Unconscious Choking	5 chest compressions, look, 2 breaths-adult/child/infant
Rescue Breaths	Normal Breath given over 1 second until chest rises
Chest Compressions to Ventilation Ratios (Single Rescuer)	30:2 – Adult/Child/Infant
Chest Compressions to Ventilation Ratios (Two Rescuer)	30:2 – Adult 15:2 – Child/Infant
Chest Compression rate	About 100/minute – Adult/Child/Infant
Chest Compression Land marking Method	Simplified approach – center of the chest – Adult/Child 2 or 3 fingers, just below the nipple line at the center of the chest - Infant
AED	1 shock, then 2 minutes (or 5 cycles) of CPR
Anaphylaxis	Assist person with use of prescribed auto injector
Asthma	Assist person with use of prescribed inhaler

- Check the scene
- Check for responsiveness – ask, "Are you OK?"
- Adult - call 911, then administer CPR
- Child/Infant – administer CPR for 5 cycles, then call 911

- Open victim's airway and check for breathing – look, listen, and feel for 5 - 10 seconds
- Two rescue breaths should be given, 1 second each, and should produce a visible chest rise
- If the air does not go in, reposition and try 2 breaths again
- Check victim's pulse – chest compressions are recommended if an infant or child has a rate less than 60 per minute with signs of poor perfusion.
- Begin 30 compressions to 2 breaths at a rate of 1 breath every 5 seconds for Adult; 1 breath every 3 seconds for child/infant
- Continue 30:2 ratio until victim moves, AED is brought to the scene, or professional help arrives

AED

- ADULT/ Child over 8 years old - use Adult pads
- Child 1-8 years old – use Child pads or use Adult pads by placing one on the chest and one on the back of the child
- Infant under 1 year of age - AED not recommended

Special Report: Recommended Daily Allowances

Compound	Units	Adult	Adult	Children	Infants	Pregnant	Lactating+
		Males (25+years)	Females (25+years)	4-8 years	6-12 mos.		
Biotin	Mcg	30*	30*	12*	6*	30*	35*
Calcium (Ca)	Mg	1200*	1200*	800*	270*	1000*	1000*
Chloride (Cl)	Mg	750	750	600	300	750	750
Chromium (Cr)	Mcg	50-200	50-200	50-200	20-60	50-200	50-200
Copper (Cu)	Mg	1.5-3	1.5-3	1-2	0.6-0.7	1.5-3	1.5-3
Fluoride (F)	Mg	4*	3*	1*	0.5*	3*	3*
Folate	Mcg	400*	400*	200*	80*	600*	500*
Iodine(I)	Mcg	150	150	120	50	175	200
Iron (Fe)	Mg	10	(25-50y) 15(51+y) 10	10	10	30	15
Magnesium (Mg)	Mg	420**	320**	130**	75*	350-400**	310-360**
Manganese (Mn)	Mg	2-5	2-5	2-3	0.6-1.0	2-5	2-5
Molybdenum (Mo)	Mcg	75-250	75-250	50-150	20-40	75-250	75-250
Niacin	Mg	16**	14**	8**	4*	18**	17**
Pantothenic	Mg	5*	5*	3*	1.8*	6*	7*
Phosphorus (P)	Mg	700**	700**	500**	275*	700**	700**
Potassium(K)	Mg	2000	2000	1600	700	2000	2000
Protein	G	63	50	28	14	60	65
Selenium (Se)	Mcg	70	55	30	15	65	75
Sodium (Na)	Mg	500	500	400	200	500	500
Vitamin A	mcgRE*	1000	800	700	375	800	1300
Vitamin B1(Thiamine)	Mg	1.2**	1.1**	0.6**	0.3*	1.4**	1.5**
Vitamin B2 (Riboflavin)	Mg	1.3**	1.1**	0.6**	0.4*	1.4**	1.6**
Vitamin B6 (Pyridoxine)	Mg	1.7**	1.5**	0.6**	0.3*	1.9**	2.0**
Vitamin B12 (Cyanocobalamin)	mcg	2.4**	2.4**	1.2**	0.5*	2.6**	2.8**
Vitamin C	Mg	60	60	45	35	95	90
Vitamin D	mcg	(51-70y) 10*(71+y) 15*	(51-70y) 10*(71+y) 15*	(1-8y) 5*	5*	5*	5*
Vitamin E	Mgalpha TE*	10	8	7	4	12	11
Vitamin K	mcg	80	65	30	10	65	65
Zinc (Zn)	Mg	15	12	10	5	15	19

Special Report: Additional Bonus Material

Due to our efforts to try to keep this book to a manageable length, we've created a link that will give you access to all of your additional bonus material.

Please visit http://www.mometrix.com/bonus948/nsca to access the information.